Something is very wrong with the government

By

Dean Moriarty

Copyright 2016

Distributed by Amazon and Kindle

FORWORD

How much are we served in the games played where the two faces of evil are the only choice, where on the one hand is the great lie held as truth and on the other is the soul sold for money?

How did this come to be deserved? Is the subjective soul to be blamed for choosing this, or is there something more sinister happening where the land of the free is but a cliché in the land of the bought and paid for, and slaves all to the system that serves only the wealthy?

Are we beginning to wake up to the choices that are given and at last to step back from it all and find the real choices that include none of the above? Our destiny cannot be left up to those who care nothing for it.

It's not too late; there is another way if only we can find it.

Today is a good day that lasts all day long.

It is said that the bottom is a part of the top without which there would be no in-between, but to those in the know there is no top or bottom, there is only where you are now.

Are we fighting to believe that what there is to believe in is true regardless of all the evidence to the contrary?

The psychology we are looking for is the one that fits all contradictions, so choose love, it's everywhere.

Death is the absence of life in something that had life, and when you see it you realize it is only a moving on and a leaving behind of the carcass that is rotting down, and that has nothing more to do with you, for all you knew of it has gone.

Today we have the beginning of the change we are looking for to happen for things to become in-line to allow our dreams to come into being. For those that have dreams this is a good time, for those that don't it can be a time of turmoil, but then, today is like that with its promise it can be so.

Let us move on from all the forms of oppression that hold us back.

CHANGE, OR THE STATUS QUO?

On the other hand peace can happen at the drop of a hat, with no further explanation than is happening. I believe it is this possibility that is spreading throughout the subjective consciousness and is becoming a mainstream awakening to more and more of us and is causing no little concern to those at the top of the pile.

It is possible that measures have been implemented to cause mass fear to stop this awakening, to keep the status quo as is to preserve the way of life for a select few that rule over us.

Peace would be their undoing and so their rhetoric is full of the promises you want to hear and ways to combat the enemy.

Anyone sane enough will see through all this and know there is no enemy, we all live on the same planet, and that wars are created for profit and fear mongering to keep us divided and seeing others as the enemy.

Those that caused the wars and are now deceiving us yet again into voting them in to cause more of the same, and have made the choice little more than choosing the lesser of two evils.

Time to wake up, stand back from it all and choose another way.

They are afraid this and will do al in their power to keep us ensnared in their game where even if you don't believe in their lies you will feel compelled to vote for them in fear of the alternative that is portrayed as much worse.

If you really want change then be the change you want.

HOW DID THEY GET INTO POWER OVER US?

It seems so obvious to me that what they do is not right, that when they take the support from the poor and disabled just so they the government have more money to give to the already well-off, well, something is seriously wrong.

How did they get into power?

Why was their corruption not seen when it was time to vote for them, and if they lied to get into power then why didn't enough people know they were lying? Were they so devious they hoodwinked the voters so easily or perhaps it was that they had a secret agenda to be implemented after getting into power but until that time came they believed their own lies and so seemed genuine?

Or perhaps more sinister still, did the ones that really control the government string them and the public along until it was too late?

And now it is so hard to get them out, to stop them.

It seems they are not accountable to the people of this country, they won't listen to us and carry on regardless; so if they are not accountable to us then who are they accountable to?

Why are they targeting the disadvantaged? Why are the rich not taxed fairly? Why does everyone feel so powerless to make change for the better? Why is the anger of so many not being addressed? Why do the rich keep getting richer, while the poor are kept poor? Why is austerity becoming worse while the government laugh their heads off and give themselves huge pay rises and take so much? Why are they not paying for the austerity measures that they instigated and perpetuate? Who or what do we owe so much to, and why do we have to pay, and keep on paying?

The government award themselves huge bonuses, which means they are a corporation of businessmen and not really a government of the people. Who decided to implement this and when did it come about?

If there is so little money for the things we need in this country then where is the money coming from for all the bombs to drop on the people of other countries that this government is so proud of?

Why is this government so keen to begin and perpetuate wars that benefit no one but the government and the arms dealers who live in luxury so far from any wars?

Where is the justice? What happened to their humanity?

Is this government so drugged and out of touch with reality that they have become insane?

Madness can be defined as a sickness of spirit that causes illusion that is believed to be real that is acted upon and causes harm to self and or others.

Are madmen in power over us?

If we are ruled by the insane that have no accountability then we are all in big trouble.

AMERICA, LAND OF THE CROOKED?

So, it's been proved that the elections are rigged and the one who stood to gain by that has won. And now, instead of demanding a re-vote she is seen to be praised for this and will be voted for because she is the lesser of two evils.

And as more and more of the crookedness, corruption etc, and lies come to light, still she is voted for because she's better than Trump, you say, and she knows what she's doing.

Really?

With her emails alone she either didn't know and that makes her incompetent, or she did know and that makes her incompetent.

Trump is Trump and no one really knows what he will be like as president yet the mainstream propaganda against him is believed.

The world is at war and Hillary will be voted for because she says things are good and getting better and so she will keep the status quo as is; but things are only good for her and those at the top, and those at the top have just paid 400 millions in unmarked bills to the terrorists.

If corruption is seen to win in America then the whole world will see this, and how can't that be good?

Wake up everyone and stop believing the lies; they can't be trusted, their record shows this.

Bring back Bernie Sanders and show the world how great America is and that America really is the land of the free.

THE DODGY DAVES OF THIS WORLD

In the deeps of our betterment they say as the government is hard at work and will not take no for an answer.

I cannot say more what I have said not although I can elaborate until the cows come home what isn't said, and if what isn't said is said more of, then much will be said about nothing; and talking such becomes the whispering rain that puts us to sleep. So when all has been said about this which is never any time soon the mouth can be closed, but if the mouth is open and words still pour out the end hasn't been reached.

This is why politicians go to sleep while listening to other politicians pour out their perpetual drivel that never ends and means nothing and used only to fill the allotted time until they can punch out and put in their request for another hand-out from the public purse, and by their own reasoning are scroungers of the system that supports them.

These perpetual scroungers are parasites that fill their own pockets and have no regard for anyone but themselves and are a drain on the hard working people of this country.

They are overpaid for their so called worth which is mostly worthless. These few that owe so much to so many are all that is wrong with the country they leach off and as a sub-species their time has come to step aside as the Neanderthals they are and let those with honour, truth and compassion replace them.

Their dishonesty and disregard for public opinion and concern to the extent that they laugh their heads off at the joke they see it all as is appalling and makes a mockery of their position as government of this country.

Just knowing these so called leaders are in power and are taking all they can while they can is depressing and brings no joy of any kind and even to write about them and their crimes brings little satisfaction, but I will not be silent any longer and let them get away with it.

The time has come to speak out and expose them for what they really are. They are clever and tricky and have the wealth and power to deflect where the focus should be, and in their deviousness are seen as something more than what they are; they hoodwink the public into believing they are upright, honest and hard working for the betterment of the country as a whole while in secret behind everyone's backs their greed knows no bounds.

Their lies are glossed over as a miner oversight in the great scheme of things that will one day see us all better off when the austerity measures end and the wars have made the world into a peaceful and safe place to be.

But the austerity measures and wars keep them and their chums in wealth and power and will never end until they are stopped and replaced with sanity in the form of a government that has the good of the people at heart, and from what I can see from where I am Jeremy Corbyn is the only worthwhile candidate to welcome in a new government for the people and of the people.

Where did we go so wrong? We didn't; we trusted and were misled and betrayed by those that took advantage of our trust, that lied about their promises just to get into power and once in went about doing whatever they pleased to further their own ends to the detriment of anyone not rich, and never before has so much been owed by so few to so many.

Do we fall off the bone for this and let the Dodgy Daves get away with it, or do we all rise up as one and find a way to get them out. Enough is enough and it is clear we are not all in this together.

THEY ARE AFRAID OF US

They have so much to lose that even in their crumbling arrogance their fear of us cannot be contained and shows in their failing system, and as humanity awakens their fear grows.

Many are waking up now, too many for them to silence so they resort to mass surveillance, banning public protests as they have done in Spain, with huge police presence in the ones still allowed ready to clamp down on any protest that looks as if it can't be controlled, and even inciting riots so they can move in and break it up.

They know what is going on and have equipped the police with all that they need to break up protests that are too threatening, and of course any and that means most protests that are not in their interests are not made known to the wider public.

TV and newspapers that are controlled do not report the protests so that those still asleep stay asleep and don't get any ideas something is going on, that the world is rising up against the corrupt systems, and those who suspect and are half awake are stuck in apathy, fear and poverty.

People-power can only do so much, and as they tighten down on us and without a leader to focus, this protesting energy dissipates.

In two of the most powerful systems, the USA and the UK, Bernie Sanders and Jeremy Corbyn have come to the fore and although not perfect offer a semblance of sanity in what can only be seen as the madness of greed and power in a world gone so crazy it is on the brink of chaos that threatens us all.

There is a lot of anger built up from years of oppression and there are those who would use this anger in a violent way, but this does more harm than good and turns any public sympathy away from their cause and only helps to make the system stronger as it turns against them and this makes it harder for everyone else as government surveillance becomes tighter, the rights of people become more eroded and the police state becomes ever more oppressive to the extent that marshal law is almost upon us as a way of life.

It has been said that false flags of destruction are caused by those in power to increase power through fear over us to the extent that everyone is watched, and any deviation from the norm is quickly pounced upon and squashed and in some cases the perpetrators are killed to remove the perceived threat and cause more fear.

So where is the hope in all this?

Should the legal tax avoidance schemes for the rich be scrapped worldwide so that there is so much money coming in the austerity measures can be stopped?

Should a fairer system of government be implemented so that the concerns of society as a whole will be listened to and addressed?

Should all the wars be stopped and all troops be brought home and all meddling in other countries affairs be withdrawn?

Should government and media be open and transparent and be accountable to the people they should be serving?

Should poverty be addressed as a matter of urgency, perhaps with the implementation of universal income?

Should prisons turn from big incarceration and money making hell-holes into places where people can be helped to turn away from crime and wrong thinking and discover their worth?

Should we as a species realize that this planet is home to all of us, that we all live here together, that there is no division among us but what has been made up to keep us divided, and that we can all live here in peace if that is what we all choose?

And where is peace? Peace is inside every one of us, not as an absence of war but as a feeling in the heart that has always been there, and that when we turn to it, it will welcome us home.

And as a wise man once said: blessed are the peace makers for they will be called the children of god.

KEEP HOPE ALIVE

Does no one see the disparity of a Nobel peace prize winner dropping huge amounts of bombs to kill people in the name of peace, while those who actively promote peace are not heard of in the news outlets?

Is it not appallingly strange that the supposed 'land of god' commits huge atrocities against its neighbour and the land of the peace prize bomber supports them?

Why are so many protesting all over the world against their own governments that are supposed to be the voice of the people they represent but after getting into power drop that pretence and pursue their own agenda that is usually the agenda of the acquisition of money?

Why is it so almost impossible to get rid of the corrupt governments after they get into power?

The rich and powerful give lip service to some wrathful god, but in their hearts they worship the gods of money and power over all else; is this not the definition of pure hypocrisy?

Does no one find it too strange that the wealthy can open their mouths and spew out unreasonable garbage and it is spread far and wide, yet those voices for sanity are not heard on the wider stage?

Ignorance and poverty is a disease of humanity that is spread over the entire world, which is actively promoted by ones whose interest it serves, while the cure for ignorance is hidden in disinformation and does not serve their interests. An informed and aware people surely could never allow such disparity of justice of all that's good to continue.

Orwell's 84 is here and its insidious message is it is too late to stop it. Yet there is hope, and for some it is hope alone that keeps them going.

So if you have hope, then keep it alive somehow, for without hope we are finished and darkness will prevail.

There is a battle for the hearts and minds of everyone, for the greater good they will say, but the greater good only benefits the rich and powerful to the detriment of everyone else, yet they would have you believe the opposite.

Your heart and mind belong to you so use them wisely and understand the intrinsic value of your own being that can be found in your own heart. It is there, so keep hope alive until it is revealed to you.

We all have our disparate demons to confront, inside and out, and when first confronted grow huge to frighten us back into submission, so it takes a certain amount of courage to hold your own and be aware, that all that is not of you, will fall away, and all that is you will come to the light until you stand in your own power and feel your own heart and think your own thoughts and hope can grow strong and that there is justice in this existence that is insurmountable to the gods of fear, greed, ego, anger and lust, and that there are those on this planet that are bringing peace to quench that thirst we all have that has been buried so deep it seems so hard to find.

Never give up, there is hope. And in the words of another wise one: never lose your hope for a pocket full of snake.

TICKET TO UNRAVEL

Old men, bored with their being rule the world and make the rules to turn all in their favour; but their favour is passionless and all they say dribbles dead from their lips and strangles them as they fade into their apathy with nothing left to offer but sickness and twisted thinking they would put upon everyone else.

So give me one more cigarette with all this writing on the wall that leaves me aghast at it all.

But life is not supposed to make you cry; and has anyone noticed that it is the mouth when opened that makes all the noise.

Oh how much we hide ourselves; how we're afraid to show our real selves in the masks that fit so tight.

The shadow of my soul as a string-less love affair began to empty as I dared still, partly under the sun and partly asking to be found.

As I unravelled I saw my making revealed as a shimmer of light dancing for me just out of reach, so I gave it my heart and was accepted.

This is a crossword puzzle that has no name. It comes from sublime and pieces of same; leg of a chair, bag of the chips, get me to heaven before I go blip.

If only my teeth were pure enough to chomp through this movement that brings so much of what I can't deal with anymore.

Doing things I can't take home; writing about the dust in the dust, as the snowdrops of your love fade in my memory.

To live where no doors will open can seem a curse, and to continue living there could see you screaming in despair.

Long is the night so dark and empty is the heart separated from love, but longer still is the road to freedom so far from home.

IF I STARE AT THES SUN TOO LONG

If I stare at the sun too long will I really go blind? They tell me so many things and so many of them have been disproved it's hard to believe anything they say anymore.

A while back I decided to disbelieve everything they say until it is proved as an indisputable fact beyond doubt.

Who are they, I mean really, who are they, and where do they all keep coming from? There seems to be some kind of fat-cat machine that churns them out, and they're all good for nothing, not one is a farmer or a nurse or something useful like that, they all seem to be from some economics or law factory where they're robotically programmed to believe in the god of money and the law of the rich; when was the last time that one of them went to prison for stealing a sandwich?

And the stink they're making of the planet can be tasted everywhere; there seems to be no escape from them, nowhere you can go to live free of their influence, not one place that isn't polluted by their corruption and greed.

They look down with their eyes in the sky and their big bombs and tell us the world is safer; safer from what? Throughout history they are the ones who have started all the wars, and they say they are the civilised ones and that they must preserve their way of life at all costs as they hide behind their huge walls while the terror they create comes among us to do so much harm. And afterwards they run the numbers up and say who the bad ones are and they are who we must fight with their war machine, while all the while they gobble down their fat food and laugh their heads off at all the harm they've caused, safe behind their huge walls paid for and built by us.

And they're so entrenched in their power base they can't be touched or held accountable, not yet anyway, maybe one day when enough of us wake up to know what's going on.

So I stare at the sun and wonder if I'll go blind before the answer comes.

COME TO BE BROKEN

Fortunately there is something more than all the lies and deceit and we all have it inside us to turn to when we are ready...

When the breast of a woman becomes illegal then we are all in trouble...

If you can't find the man in the moon then you've never been to Neptune...

Let me put it this way: when you get to the end you have only just begun....

An old alligator crawled into the space that was left behind from before...

"Can we confirm this?" said the confirmation society riding their broomsticks into the wind of all that would be confirmed...

"I'm not sure," said the inner goddess called Mary the Aphrodite who was creeping up on the be-Jesus of it all...

"You must not leave me behind," said the alligator...

"Never mind," said never mind.

And then it was time to go home at the end of the day and the game was over...

...or perhaps I should put it another way: there is no way it can be put...

So when I put it like that there is nothing more to be said...

..And then the rain comes down to soak you until you dance in the wet of it all...

I see you speaking your truth...and from this you are seen to be what you are...

...and not unkind, you bow before the storm that comes at you...

Come, this will break you...

...and moving you to move the way inside you find all becomes the magic dust you thought long lost beside a road you forgot about in all the forgetting that came and went inside this that came and went...

On that shore where once we met and came apart in all we held to be so, we loved, and knew something of ourselves to be true...

...but the flow is something that takes us on, and moving on we lose touch with all that is past and gone...

...and more is but a memory that can't be reached anymore...

Don't really know what's going on; in this plane of existence things are other. Your lips are strange tonight where we thought we were, we are not. I thought it was you but now I know it was not...

Never mind, blame it on the government.

TIME OUT

I guess that's what we are all asking, give us time out from your death plans. But they don't listen; they expect quarter in the war they make yet give no mercy. They couldn't care less about the deaths they've caused.

It seems they are deliberately going about systematically getting rid of the weak, the disabled and the less well-off; the same as Hitler did when he tried to exterminate the Jews and the gypsies and other undesirables in the making of his perfect society.

All of which makes me wonder if we really did win the last world war, or did the evil ones just re-group and are now at it again with the same master plan implemented as their own.

What else is there to think when you look at history and see it horribly repeating itself?

And all those brave ones who fought to bring us freedom from tyranny only bought us a reprieve with their lives. The war to end all wars they said, with the next big one should have been a wake-up call to humanity that something is very wrong somewhere.

Too often the next world war almost begins, but the fear is that if it does then no one would survive and there would be nothing left to come out to from the bunkers.

If it was just one Dodgy Dave that we were all against we would have little to be concerned about because his time in power is over; the trouble is he would be replaced by another just as bad, and we will have to begin over again until all of them are out and for good and a humane government put in their place.

This island we live on is home to a proud and independent people who have stood against tyranny and prevailed and whose identity is like no other.

All this and more has been eroded by being a part of the corporation of the EU which is far too costly in more ways than one; and whatever benefits we may have by being a part of it are far outweighed by what it costs us all to remain in it, and ideologies aside, if it was going to work for the betterment of the whole it would have done so by now and we would see that, but it is failing and is only being propped up by the unsustainable economy that is running out of time.

The mistakes of the past don't have to define us; we can go forward with hope and set aside the old paradigms that are failing and see past the lies and deceit and bring about change that will benefit all of us.

So I say time out, time out from the Dodgy Daves of this world; time out from the failing capitalism, from the unsustainable growth programmes, from the inhumanity, from the ignorance and death and destruction that is so wide-spread.

Just time-out so that peace can take a hold and we can all breathe a sigh of relief, so that we can all thrive and find the joy of being alive on our beautiful Earth, this most amazing place that is our home.

And if there are wise words that could implement a time-out from all this, I for one would like to hear them.

SOMETHING TO BE DEPRESSED ABOUT

And then, the time had come for the great tidy-up as a slow death spread over the land that came from machines paid for by the government to spread it far and wide where only the weak and old would be affected to die of some cancer that would be incurable after taking the expensive cure from the pharmaceutical company.

The government of course were safe on holiday, by design and were laughing it up as the rest of us breathed in the fumes.

The evil ones looked down from their ivory towers as the master plan progressed and was so far along by now it was said that not even a miracle could stop it.

Only the well-off were to be given any help to become more wealthy, all others were workers in the production lines of the economy and programmed to obey and to toe the line of the party politics set out for them.

Everyone had their place in this scheme except the non-productive ones, the sick, the lame and the disabled who were to be eliminated to make room for those to come who would be schooled according to their ability to fit into the machine of productivity.

Lies and deceit were the norm and seen as truth; everyone had their version of the lie to vote for and encouraged by the propaganda machines, the TVs, newspapers etc to believe it all and live accordingly.

Laws were passed to outlaw homelessness to drive them all off the streets. Other laws were passed to outlaw protesting in large numbers, and one by one the countries of the world incorporated this into the system.

All heart based feelings were unlearned in the belief systems taught over the propaganda machine; sympathy was only for the devil, a deviant and subversive whose only place was as a scare tactic to keep the religious in line.

And God as some perpetuated myth that everyone believed in, who lived up there in the clouds had an angry wrath that would kill you dead in a heartbeat if you didn't obey the rules.

Control became ever tighter as fear was spread of terrorism and shown to be so by well-orchestrated bombings to instil the fear deeper and deeper.

Disinformation was used to cause confusion and any who saw through it all were branded subversives and disposed of when the time was right.

Peace and freedom were words used by the war machine to give the hope that one day, in some utopian future when the austerity measures finally ended and the last of the terrorists were rounded up and jailed wealth would come down to us all so that we all could live safe in our little boxes of consumerism and conformity without fear as our leaders worked hard on our behalf to keep it that way.

And in the words of an old philosopher: if you can't think for yourself you'll think for them.

THE MASKS WE WEAR

When something is looked at for the first time it is seen for how it is, but constant looking at it builds up an image in our mind and it is this image that has been built up that is seen and not the thing that is looked at.

This familiarity is one aspect of the masks we build up over time; some of the masks are forced upon us by society, in the schools we went to, by our family, friends and culture to name a few.

Take language for instance: in childhood we absorb how others say things in a certain way and so we mimic them and learn phrases and ways of speaking that are used over and over and often in this way we lose the art of thinking for ourselves, or never really learn it.

Our minds have tracks to run along, well used expressions that are fallen back on and become our way of communicating. It is not until awareness happens perhaps from travelling away from the familiar is all this realized and the form broken out of which usually happens in an organic awakening over a period of time as you become more aware of the confines of linear or system thinking.

It's a strange thing, the masks that are worn over all to portray an illusion, and the funny thing is, although the masks hide the real inside, it also clouds the outside seeing by the very act of wearing them and seeing through them.

When the mask slips momentarily, things are seen for what they are, clearly, and sometimes this can come as a shock and cause fear, to be losing control of a long held reality only to find it was never real but only the perceptions of our upbringing and culture.

When the mask is taken off it can be likened to another dimension where things are the same, yet not the same and are seen as they are and not coloured by the layers of the mask.

Some drugs will blast you right out of your comfort zone into be here and now of it all but can be a harsh shock to the system.

Meditation on the other hand will give you an awakening but in a gentle way where you unfold at your own pace and can feel the masks dropping away as you find your way back to yourself.

For some, the masks they wear are taken for who they are and confusion happens when anything comes to expose this belief and often the masks are put on tighter to uphold their way of seeing things.

It is a cause of increasing concern to more and more people that those who are governing society wear the biggest masks of all and are being seen as the blind leading the blind.

To be seemingly lost in an inescapable illusion of conformity must feel like a straight-jacket that confines the soul in the mundane circles of perpetuated beliefs and repetitive thinking that is such a distance from our authentic selves.

The consciousness of humanity is rising and the masks are slipping off one by one as awareness of who we are is becoming known to more and more; and those who hang onto their masks will be seen for what they are by those who have taken the mask off.

It can be difficult to remove the familiar mask that has been for so long how we have seen our-self through and has been our protection against the harsh reality we would be protected from.

We will find our-self vulnerable without the mask as a creature suddenly exposed to the sunlight, or for some it will be a doorway they go through into a magical place.

Those still wearing masks will throw judgement and ridicule and dismissal at those without a mask, but with courage, this very vulnerability will be strength to live a life of integrity that comes from a place of love where the mind has finally quieted enough for the heart to be heard.

OLD PARADIGMS

There are elements of old paradigms yet remaining with a lot of power and influence that would keep the intelligence and consciousness levels of the vast majority of humans considerably restricted to preserve the way of life of those at the top.

Things are changing so fast at an exponential rate a great awakening is going on and to the ones who have awakened enough nothing can be hidden and even though huge attempts have been made to dumb down the populace to keep them in their place as slave workers and consumers still, the universal consciousness level is rising which must be causing some consternation and fear to those very few who are in seemingly invincible and unassailable power over us, which makes them even more dangerous than they're ever been.

And so this is an attempt to address this imbalance to explain with quantum entanglement in such a way it can be understood for what it is by the ordinary person in the street, even though their attention spans have been disturbed like hot molecules to boil over at the least little thing.

Quantum theory, so named is but something that has been studied and known for thousands of years and the current modern theories are but explanations of what was already known long ago.

Such as the Buddhist theory that time and space are but constructs of the mind and that solid form is an illusion that is made up of whirling patterns with more space in between these whirling patterns than was previously thought; and also that everything is connected by an invisible force that can't be measured.

So if time, space and form are not real then what is?

So, do we keep on saying: 'pay unto Caesar what is Caesar's, or do we finally remove the ignorance that is sucking the lifeblood from humanity?'

Fear, as in fear of reprisal and condemnation may make you hesitate.

Condemnation from the religious authorities and reprisal from the state policy; between these two humanity has been kept repressed for centuries and maybe even far longer and who knows how much advancement we all could have made if greed and religious persecution had not come about.

If we come into being for but a moment as an illusion to experience uniquely an existence of form, and having seen to return, the form back into the dust leaving behind a small ripple that fades back into stillness, what then is our existence for?

Is it a self determined course we make for ourselves to eventually awaken and become enlightened or are we here for something else? And if we can't find it are we losers to be ridiculed; and if we follow one path for an age and still find no higher plane of existence beyond the mundane, have we failed?

For like this we are lost; and I hear your voices; and I would tend to agree with you if my bed wasn't burnt to a cinder long ago.

Generally speaking, what you see is what you get, but what you see is not all there is, so, on the one hand it might be said: what is the use of knowing this, and on the other hand you might say the use is in the knowing.

Brief is the love that comes to play sometimes, and quickly it slips away unnoticed; and sorry is the one who lets it go and tired to try again yet hoping for the heroism to feel where even in the aloneness we are not so alone; and a long way from heaven we are where we wear our feet so low and our splendour oven lower.

Small is the night without love and long are the hours to endure; and then to cry in the small hours of your love when you find your love is not so big; and all the Herculean endeavours have come to less than nothing, and less than that you feel so small in such a huge place where no physics can ever penetrate so deep to raise you up.

So the question is, do we carry on into the void, perhaps not even hoping anymore to find that heart, or do we turn back, or, if all seems lost then perhaps to just give up; and all this seen under a spectral kaleidoscope and is kind of like nailing down an onion on the edge of Jupiter with a piece of coloured crystal.

The gamma gallows theory leaves much to be desired.

WHEN THE BALLOON WENT UP

The early morning graffiti was still half asleep in the shadows of the rising sun where two pints of Mary had gone the night before in the recondite recognition of a lowly wall.

Up through the tide of day it pushed with its brash statement that the sea levels were on the rise too fast and we are all doomed.

A motion stone that had no boundaries and rarely took prisoners became enamoured with the graffiti and took it to heart as a prophesy and so began planning to build a boat.

When news got on the grapevine that something was happening the bible thumpers banged on their bibles like monkeys in the jungle and all began babbling at once that the second coming was close and to get to church to pray harder for salvation.

When the government were questioned about the coming apocalypse it was denied, but behind closed dark doors secret meetings happened where they all laughed their heads off and talked in gobbledygook (politician style) until the balloon went up and then they all fell asleep; it all being too much for them to comprehend, and one of the alcoholics was kind enough to die of liver failure (politician style of course.

Into the equation more and more enlightened ones came to put the fire out, and although the universe didn't care one way or the other about any of it, still they did their best and a voice was heard here and there before it was extinguished by the evil ones with their long shadows that spread over all the land.

So it was little wonder that so many in disguise wrote on walls their truth and then went back into hiding.

Many were lost in the wars, in their sex and religion, in front of TVs, and the institutions they fitted into that ate them and left so little behind to talk to it was hardly worth the bother.

Strange is the world and stranger still is the spaghetti graffiti that spread over all the walls of all the cities until they were all covered and there was nothing left to say.

THE BROOM CLOSET OF DOOM

The untapped source of what everyone was here for was tapping the source of what everyone was doing with not a lot happening and not getting very far. So much beer was sent out for and a jolly good time was had drinking it until the cows came tapping home to be milked.

Sunny Money was always a good sport and never stopped talking, even when her mouth was shut and so found herself the centre of attention most times and seemed to need it.

The curse of doom on the other hand was always asking for too much and gave nothing away but knew how to tap the source better than anyone that anyone knew which is what everyone wanted to know and so paid it lots for its formula that didn't work for anyone but it, and so everyone blamed themselves and kept going back to it and giving it more money hoping something would rub off onto them, but who can look in the face of doom and not shrivel up.

Behind the gates of this where the cobwebs talked to themselves and the shadows on the wall kept them company where too nothing could be said that made any sense the thin line of the morning sun was being drawn in the sand to stand behind to make a stand against all that could be stood against that was left to stand against notwithstanding the veil that was barely standing and was about to lift to let in the light and show everyone the way home, that is if there was anyone left standing by then; anyway, behind the gates of this understanding no more could be said which is not saying much but a lot can be made up if you tap hard enough.

And so with this Sunny Money ran off as fast as her legs would go and disappeared forever from the curse of doom; but the cords of attachment were long and not broken so easily. And so the curse of doom found her hiding in the vault where the rich kept their money and blowing bubbles to her heart's content.

"Splendid, I've found you," said the curse of doom and heaved the heavy sack of all her troubles from off his shoulder and dumped it on the floor by her feet where it began to inch back into her life without so much as a by your leave or a written invitation.

Far away and down below in the dungeon that was closer to hell but further from the truth by design the unborn again was practicing being grateful for all his troubles which was a long shot in anyone's game but was worth a try, and what else was there to do anyway; and so began wailing for all he was worth.

When sound of the wailing reached the king's ears a decree was immediately made by royal command that from now on all wailing must be done in silence so as not to offend the king in his castle.

"Some people have no respect," said the king and made it so.

Day and night tongues were cut out until all the wailing in the castle became silent and the king could finally get a good night's sleep.

A Bavarian monk passing by on his way to find a quiet cave on a mountain top liked the quiet of the castle so much he moved in and became the most silent there, but as he didn't speak no one ever knew.

Because Sunny Money wouldn't marry the king and had run off, her brother and most of her family were being tortured to death for the king's amusement, but the king had grown bored as kings do and had taken to his bed to utter nonsense in his sleep which was all written down by the truth tellers who never slept.

Over in the coal mine big Ming was executing his escape routine and had too much on his mind to give a comment at this time and so was let off the hook and given a parking ticket instead.

Not to be outdone by any of this the creased face of an old stamp without a hope in hell and boring the legs off of anyone who came close tried hard to say more of what couldn't be said more of and all things considered said quite a bit: "Do I ask for so much in my existing and am I as worthless as the dust? And defeated at last in the asking where so much is ungiven not a word more can be uttered or it will seem that I am ungrateful for my lot."

And with that no more was said.

The broom in the corner that was not so squeamish picked up on this and began to recite its litany of regret: "So much effort and asking and so many, many days long and short, remembered and lost to get past the breaking point of the heart in pain only to become another wayward wanderer no longer wandering and so lost in the losing to give up all hope and mark time until in the dust of passing all striving ceases and life is gone."

The basket weaver wasn't listening and perhaps it was for the best, for who knows what a broom would become if it rose above its station to become something else.

IN THE LAND OF THE BLIND

When the king woke up all his sin was forgiven him and so he was able to go to breakfast a new man and wonder again why his table was so empty of anything that could spare him from his doom.

The curse of doom was very busy in the king's kingdom and ran around with free reign to plunder all it could and strike up bargains all over the place with all the poor souls living in austerity and who paid such heavy taxes and such for the rich to live in luxury.

The rich complained they were a small hard done by minority and so made up laws to ban the poor from grumbling about their lot and blaming the rich. They also made up lies that were spread everywhere so that the poor didn't know if they were coming or going most of the time which helped to keep them in their place in fear and working hard.

Depression moved in over the land and struck left right and centre and many fell to this affliction and so were given drugs to cure them but the drugs only made things worse.

All this of course was a small part of the master plan of the unconvicted felons who were the real rulers of the land and had no regrets and were trying to live forever so that they never died; and so used their wealth to that end.

On the shop floor of all this and outback of any hope that could be, Mandy Marbles was lying in the dust with nothing better to do than scratch her many ant bites and complain that her story was not going the way she wanted it to.

Zen on the other hand was fighting hard and pushing back the doom if it all and was extremely busy all things considered, so never let it be said there was no balance in the land.

THE GRAVEROBBERS HOLE

So when the big Mumbles, the basket weaver and the boon-dock wailer got to Cleveland on the 06.40 out of Penn they set up shop in the conversion frequencies to buy time and spread it about with their tongues on fire to all and sundry and hoped that the little bitter was not lurking in the shadows to jinx them again and drive them out of another town.

Driving south in a car made of many late hours and a rusty spanner and spreading the dawn for a change was the audience of all expectation and a free-loader to boot, give or take a shake of the dog's tail in the back seat that had nothing much better to do than count its chewed bones.

In the grip of going too far and not a moment out of time the big sneeze all the way from Montana was making inroads along the very same highway of inebriation and had a wanton foot that wouldn't stay still for nothing and wanted only to feel the next breeze coming off of the ocean of freedom where all things merge into one to find the long road home, and hallelujah to that was playing on the radio as the sun of this inspiration came up and down all by itself and never said a bad word to anyone at all, not even to the plastic banana leaf that was so tall and hanging out of the back window and waving to everyone like the ghost of everyone's favourite uncle who had finally done the impossible and escaped to fly away to that far land that had always beckoned and been ignored or put on the backburner for a time that would never come but was somehow always longed for.

Contrary to popular opinion and a footloose consciousness chaser with a taste for fried chicken on the wing and spare ribs out the back, the man in the mask who was no two ways about it most of the time and always had spare change took a wrong turn off the freeway of his design and rolled up to where the three from Penn were hammering nails into their day-glow beliefs that didn't have a hope of reaching nirvana but were enthusiastic about it for all to see and so were gathering a large crowd who all knew about the second coming and so were there to see if anything would happen in between of what wasn't there and would never be whether the dog shook its tail or not.

Rolling down his precious window of thunder he was just about to get to grips with his mouth full of teeth and call out when the holy ghost of all his old excruciations piped up and said: "Say nothing."

So with his face lost to the wind of that where the grave robbers were digging holes through his eyes and his teeth showing through his open mouth he frightened everyone into thinking that the old devil was here to take them all into the down below where it was so hard to dig your way out of.

And so with lots of arm waving and not a few screams they all ran off to hide in the back rooms of their lives where the rat-runs were so familiar and comforting.

The three from Penn stood their ground not wanting to be driven off again, but it was all too much and they gave in to their despair that never gave in to them and turned tail and ran off too, never to be seen again this side of a grave robbers hole.

Incidental to this and not overly fond of spreading rumours in the dust where the light gets in to burst out the other side a dollar over easy was sinking fast into the sunset and taking with it what could never be said in this or any other tale full of explanations driving any place to escape that terrible hole in their lives where the grave robbers lived to invite them in so much.

The fire brigade who all lived next door to this and had put out many such fires in the past of their lives had gone on strike and so were not available for comment.

Sweets for Candy and spooked on the sugar rush was coming into town the hard way but was not a one for regrets and so didn't take it personally any more than along the lines of it was all a bittersweet allusion that under it all lay the treasure that can never be found nor ever be talked about properly and so ten tons of cement would be placed over it all for the duration or until such times could be found to make sense of it.

Anyway, many words were shoe horned in edgeways like to take up the slack and it is around here that we find Sunny Money on her perch in the tree...

Sunny Money on her perch in the tree was looking down on it all to the consternation of the big Mumbles who was sitting on another branch over a-ways and hidden from spying eyes, mostly, and who was listening to ragamuffins for breakfast playing the accordion and couldn't be reached by any other line of sight than a whistle in the dark and step up with Daisy to blow me down and sneak me away and never go home again.

"Oh Sunny Money," said the old crow above her on its branch.

"Shut up," said Sunny Money sternly, "I'm trying to listen to what is being said."

WAITING FOR BREAKFAST

A small ache that was waiting for breakfast was changing lead into vinegar and had a big hole where the light got in and rattled about in there breaking all the vitreous china. There was also an umbrella floating in the wind of the penumbra that was too small to be seen but spoke in a voice of authority that no one heard.

The bus fare of this was a long ride nowhere at all with no excuse to sell anything except to fall into the drama circle of the fortune that had no plans to get married or talk French to the natives in any beat-up dawn.

And so a month went by all by itself for a whole year where a form of chilly all the way from California would not for the love of god go bluer than blue and so became a lost cause that was later found out of its mind and said it would never go back for nothing and began drinking wine that was handed down like the holy grail in the counting of its dreams that were no dreams at all but the running moment of a small ache that was waiting for breakfast.

THE END OF CORRUPTION

The graveyard closed early and went for a bottle of beer, so Sunny Money had one too and then everything began to make sense and although the oppressive doom was still lurking about somewhere, probably in the shadows, things began to look better.

The rich in their old paradigms started to die off in large numbers of doom and the king became an imbecile and was confined to his bedroom to sleep it off for the duration and in time would be forgotten as a bad dream, but not before paying restitution to all the tongue-less wailers to be set free to blink in the hot sun of their new found freedom.

Limitless Smith who'd just walked into this was having a great time of it dancing his marionette dolls at the local fair and had a suitcase full of money in his cross-hairs that was sticking out of his pocket and so was considered rich in some circles.

Everywhere he went he put a smile on people's faces and was very happy to do so and people would give him money for their pleasure and a jolly good time was had by all in the land of the imbecile king who was locked in his bedroom.

Over time, with everyone being taxed fairly, even the rich and the corporations, everyone began to thrive; even the homeless beggars had a nice house and a never went hungry.

There was such a surplus of money that everyone had a pay rise, everyone that is except the politicians and the bankers, they were all put in prison to count their evil sins until they became normal which would not be anytime soon, for their madness was deep and the only cure was no cure at all, so they were left to rot as was only fair.

The new catchphrase was: "I remember you," and it went around until there were no strangers left in the land of the blind to frighten the children; and as everyone stepped into their power the light drove out the corruption and peace was felt by everyone. This of course was the story everyone told themselves hoping it would happen.

THE LONG WINDS HOME LATER

In the perceptions perceived where the dichotic foot never stops tapping and the holy rice brigade furiously write letters of complaint furthermore to their disappointment the exception as a strange enactment of unfulfilled dreams closed the door on the distant shout of redemption, dismissed the waiting staff of their responsibilities, took out a long overdue smoke and began to pace back and fore to the tune of a sudden rainstorm that beat down hard on the tin roof of whatever sensibilities there was left and forgot about the last train of all possibilities that was due to arrive in a taxi at six PM sharp, naturally, if a little ruffled by the early hour.

The common denominator was a lucky-up if we can ever look further beyond to see more to see so much. Oh the reaching that takes us from ourselves and those stormy windows we break to get in because we have to, and entering find ourselves so alone to wait for our destiny to catch up in the leap of our doing so huge where we will be caught again saying our prayers to stay awake one last time and then off to bed with you, there's a good boy for a hail Mary and never say die, and watch out for the hole the grave-robbers leave behind, and don't forget to scrub behind your ears where the potatoes grow, and if you keep on looking at me like that you'll get a government smack to make you hop faster, and now look what you've done, you've made me lose my place; what am I going to do with you.

If the candid breakwaters of a criminal notion comes to startle you then, stand well back and do not light the touch-paper that will dangle right under your nose and call you names to provoke you until you are caught and gone and having to brave the long winds home later.

THIRTY TWO MINUTES MISSING

Thirty two minutes missing was on a hiding to nothing and was having an excellent time of it forsooth and for sure and not for all the cement in China would take no for an answer from all the missed opportunities that never came his way in the stuff of another day that had nothing to say but go back to bed.

"A mile an hour, a mile an hour," shouted out the big discrepancy going backwards slowly to the applause of the ten thousand lost in the mist.

"I am not an urgency, I am what I make myself to be," said the prisoner from his lonely grave buried so deep no one could hear him.

There was a lot of murmuring going on and not least was: "How do we fight them?" To which no answer was straightforward enough to be said.

"Don't be so small," said the magnitude earthquake and shook everyone up a bit.

Thirty two minutes missing gave up the ghost and went back to bed no wiser for his making and missed the coffee lady who came too late with the morning coffee to make any difference in the land of the blind.

Are we really that where we can't be seen, where the holy ning-ning dances and feathers fall to show us the way to go, some morphic resonance in the formulative causation?

When we rise above the collective unconsciousness we will know that where we are is not where we were, but only when we get out of here, where we're not, will we know.

A MOMENT'S WHISPER

Come September would not be realistic about being on the wrong bus
and so sat at the back with the orphans who came and went carrying
their flags of surrender and hope as if underwater and the game was
real and would remain that way until they discovered coffee and turned
off their TVs and grew beards for the revolution and meditated on the
banks of the Seine until they all turned blue for a moment's whisper to
come to rescue them and take the home again.

Some bus rides take a long time.

THE NIPPON BISCUIT COMPANY

The Nippon biscuit company were having a biscuit sale out back of beyond when a million push-less motorbikes descended out of the blue and growled to be let in, but the day was counting its chickens and eating its gruel and so said: "We shall call them by their heathen names from a distance and scarper most assuredly if they look at us the wrong way in the urban wastes of our far reaches."

"Is it such a lame biscuit to allow the young their foolishness, until their youth is swept away in concerns that come too soon and those days of carefree can only be remembered as what once was?" said the Nippon biscuit company and opened the gates and let them in.

"Suit yourself," said the day as the motorbikes roared in through the gates in a horde to mill about near the biscuit stand.

When nothing more was forthcoming the day went off to look at tiger cages in the burnt heat and took an umbrella with it, which was just as well for there are a lot of tiger cages in China.

A BRIEF APPEARANCE

The tiger cage was so lonely without a tiger to seduce so it stood in line at the bus stop for the next bus to the jungle where there were sure to be tigers.

Sometime later on the mountain top with the past just a memory the tiger cage was supping slowly a tasty soup when a shooting star looking for a new home chose that very moment to put in a brief appearance and then was gone forever.

A seagull far below on its way to the ocean missed this fly past and so carried on flying as if nothing had happened.

And as a by the way of a by the by at the foot of the mountain with his foot on the last tiger, old Jim, the burnt-down cigarette hanging out of his mouth coughed and took another drag of the thing and then threw it away and then posted the photograph of him and the dead tiger off to Tigers Monthly where it was received with much ado about nothing and put on the front page for all to see.

TAKING STOCK

When in the sometimes maybe of a long lost moment that comes back again from out of the blue a strange déjà vu is felt that it could be the time to take stock of the time.

Taking stock is an age old tradition where all the ingredients are listed in order so that you know where you are in any given moment that is slipping this way and that in the jolly-oh of it all and is sometimes confused with reality, but is most often a falling backwards to find the last time you knew where you were.

The generating engine that never sleeps may keep you awake in this, but not to worry there are things you can do to appear normal most of the time and not appear too far-out of it which is a trap in itself for then you may become stuck and this is usually far worse after the boredom sets in and with no way to escape you may find yourself waiting for a very long time for a favourable wind to come and move you on.

So be careful of taking too much stock and shake yourself out of any moments that become too long; and never let it be said in the beck and call of the too strange that you were unprepared to move mountains to find your way again to where you want to be.

Tip of the day:

On meeting the nowhere man in your travels give him a kiss and then move on fast before they make a religion out of it. And never look back or regret what you can't change, what's gone has gone and once done lives on only in your own mind, for only you can see it the way you see it.

A RUBBER TWISTED

A whisper came that the crack of doom that was the brother to the curse of doom was stealing all the money from a side door set up from before.

So Sunny Money raced to the bank to withdraw all she could but the bank was closed and wouldn't let her in.

Not to be deterred she went around the side to see for herself the side door that was being whispered about.

A slow boat full of gin, a rust bucket really stood in her way and wouldn't let her pass and became a monument to all her suffering right then which was all well and good if you were a dog and bone left in the gutter, but no use whatsoever in the free-flow five and ten that was about to crack nuts with a sledgehammer.

So breathing deeply to hold it all in she took a step backwards and then another until she was back where she started from in the towers that were no towers at all where she screamed once and then went back to blowing bubbles and wearing her rubber twisteds just in case.

A long ways off from all this in the show and tell where the days were long and enough was always near enough if you were never going to make it in the entire might of a buying spree the highly unlikely were sipping hot coffee and counting their dearly departed.

"I was never so small when I was so big," said one who spooning coffee froth into a saucer.

"Never mind dear, it'll all come back to you in the wash," said her friend trying to remember where she was and where she came from.

Under the table the curse of doom was sniggering and pulling the deluxe strings to make up a little strange for its amusement.

REBOOT

Are we robotically inclined to obey; is our programming up to date; are we affirming our beliefs; are our thoughts radicalised enough today to turn against our enemies? Or have we turned off the TV that powerful tool that is used to influence the masses to think and believe in a certain way to bring about whatever is wanted by the controllers in power?

The illusion is all encompassing and penetrates to our very essence and seems so real that people will kill to uphold it and keep it in place in the consciousness.

Anyone that speaks out against it becomes an enemy of the system, a subversive to be watched and rounded up when the time comes for the big crackdown to bring back control and neutralise the enemy.

If you think outside the proscribed boxes taught by the system and don't keep it to yourself then you will be deemed as dangerous to the system and all those enclosed within it that might be influenced by your ideas, so much so that imprisonment or even death may be used against you to control and contain you.

But they can't control everyone all of the time, just the most radical and so fear is used to keep people in check and while some letting off steam is tolerated, anyone venting too much will have a home visit and may even be taken away to one of the camps for a reboot or even a complete reprogramming.

But all this was written about long ago in Orwell's 1984 and other writings that came to warn but were ignored by the masses as more entertainment, for the government would never do that to us, we voted them in and we can vote them out, right?

So, do we feel safe in the illusion? Are we being taken care of by our masters? Do we feel in control? Are we obeying all the laws? Do we want to change anything, or are we content with the way things are?

IN-FIRMAMENT

"I will not tell you again," said the big basket weaver being far too frugal with its words in the never after all that so many were falling into every day.

"And if you don't love yourself you'll be loveless," it said as an afterthought that fell on the deaf ears of all the messiah men that were stepping forward to be counted. So it shut up and said nothing more.

"Buzz, buzz," said the candy-knickers man selling knickers.

"I will not tell you again," repeated the echo that faded away in the big hall that no one went to anymore.

The end came sooner than expected and punched a hole in the jelly-oh of the merry clappers and caused a lot of consternation that became a moot point to be cheered and then thrown in the ditch with all the other used consternations that made up all that was made up under the in-firmament; and this too became a moot point.

THE OVEN MASTERS

A bridge that the hordes were walking over fell into disrepair from over-use and so was given a D notice or the kiss of death, that the floods washed away in the government restructuring and after a while became the norm until no one noticed it wasn't there anymore; and then a drought dried the river up and they all began to cross again to the other side which was no side at all so they all turned around and went back again and so became the two way rush to nowhere until the government put up a road block and funnelled them all into a camp and bombed them all into mud.

Behind shut doors the government laughed their heads off and filled their faces with the best of everything.

When the bus came to head south the evil ones had got there first and set up a chain reaction to end all hope and turn about all those who had nowhere else to go.

And so they streamed into the land of the blind and set up camp there and the government bombed that too.

By now there were two kinds of people: the blind and the bombed that came to say: "There are many escalators of death and all of them wind up their windows against us until we are no more."

This was a turn of events that didn't bode well a happy outcome so the word happy was scratched from the dictionary and then people milled about for any outcome.

But when that didn't come about either the tables were turned to point into the wind where a big tractor was ploughing their minds into docility and the more they watched all this on TV the more servile they became until it was too late and they became sheep for the fodder and told to line up to be branded for the ovens.

The oven masters, surviving remnants of the great holocaust had turned into the master race they once hated and were so powerful no resistance could stand against them. Their war machine bombed its way outwards over the land to steal all it could as the world looked the other way just as it did when Hitler began his push that started the last world war.

AN AUDIENCE TO BOOT

The audience with one foot in the grave began to pack their bags and go home when suddenly the circles became transparent again and the dust settled and so without a backward glance digital digits and the snap-cure proof made whoopee celebrating a song in the old language in the long good night under the huge sky and not for nothing was the moon so full and beatifically hot.

Far away from all the troubles in a place called paradise in the lion's den of all you could be underneath the canopy tree:

"Err, Wilbur?"

"Si Senor?"

"What are you carrying and what is the secret password of anything?"

"Four or five kidnapped now kind of moments later:

"Give me a crate of beer senor and I will tell you everything."

"You are right; we must not sub-confine the meaning. What's that you're carrying under your arm there?"

"It is a long letter from the loony-bin senor."

"What does it say?"

"I don't know senor, I have resisted opening it."

"Perhaps I could help you with that."

"You are too kind senor."

"Think nothing of it."

THE CURE FOR DEATH

Old news from the science community said that scientists have discovered it is no longer a theory that everyone alive today will one day die if a cure is not found soon which did not please anyone at the time. But startling news has come into my possession.

A race has been going on around the clock to find a cure for death and word has filtered through that it has been discovered. A secret document has been found in a dumpster by yours truly and so I can now say without a word of doubt the cure has been found for death.

It is estimated that the pharmacological industry will charge one billion dollars per pill to each customer and already a selection committee has been set up by the government to decide who will get the pill with prominent government ministers and influential businessmen in line to receive it first.

The anti ageing pill will be designed to last one year before it breaks down and another one is needed but because the pill will reverse the effects of ageing so that the body reverts back the biological clock to the optimum age of twenty five it is considered that only four pills will be needed per century.

Recently, the gene responsible for cell decay was taken out of the DNA strand of one thousand volunteer test subjects and within a short time one hundred percent of them showed remarkable retro ageing. The prognosis is that the treatment works and is going through the final stages of testing prior to distribution to the elite who can afford it.

This is good news for the billionaires who have the funds and now can live forever and can make even more money from the consumers that are breeding at an incredible rate around the planet.

Each new consumer that comes along means money in the bank for the big corporations that are overjoyed at the news and are spreading golden handshakes in record numbers to grease the wheels to make it all happen for them.

Politicians are lining up to be bought but nothing new there; new laws are in the process.

It's a new world folks and money buys it all: power, fame, prestige, the love of many, and now immortality or everlasting life, take your pick.

History is being written as we want it and God is on our side. Nothing now can stand in our way; the new world order is here and now can't be stopped.

Plans are in place for the activists who want to spoil our fun and will shortly be rounded up and placed in control units already built for them where they can be programmed to see the error of their ways and eventually sent back out into the work pool as industrious workers and consumers, with no expense spared for their reform.

The machine is up and running and is self perpetuating. No more hiding behind the propaganda; the time is here to show who the real rulers of this planet are.

This is John Doe of the planetary enterprises group that has brought this astounding news to you all and I wish you all a very happy Christmas.

Now, where can I get a billion dollars from?

A used car anyone?

CRACKED UP TO BE

Cultural identity could be likened to mass hysteria. All form being illusion and not real and any identity with it is a kind of hypnosis such as the old boys school of us and them and so identifying with this is a form of slavery.

Realization of this is a step towards freedom and self independence away from all forms of control.

In that independence the muddied waters clear and a profound stillness occurs and is a self awareness of being that can bring great joy; but for most the school of thought is that a fancy face can go further than being half in or half out and then some between the sheets of a full bloom; but like the poor proton in the machine of the experiment blasting off is not all it's cracked up to be before sundown with a camera in your hand when the quarks are around; and now by the miraculous decision to expand we shall presume to be innocent unless questioned guilty; this is a hot-seat you can't win so plead the fifth amendment and say nothing.

This is where we occur, where we appear and most often where we are and we shall clap for the winners who have won for no reason at all but that we've let them for they've come from the hard place and must win at all costs, and it's all right, we don't mind at all; do we Miss Jones? And if we sleep forever don't wake us, we are sound where we have fallen, peeling onions in the graveyard-shift of open expansion...

Cupid's lips but this is all a typhoid fever of beauties me bucko that is the all of it all, but you are all too late and far too soon in this awakening that can't go on without you and the heart to do so, and no one else can realize you but you.

And now the fifth dimension comes to ruin a perfectly good plan I have to run into the story lines of what I have seen to say more; but I am full of erudite like a prized Indian newt full of sugar that stands without, wasting to go within, and wishing, and I am ready to fall like a

Newtonian apple right out of the sky into those quantum arms and disappear into them forever; but how can I fall that far from here where I am on the ground with no falling beneath me?

If you look closely enough through the walls you can see patterns of energy. These patterns have edges that speak, but so far all they've said to me is that the Russians are coming with their machines that can read minds and even make you think things.

I keep asking these patterns if they can be more precise but they won't say any more, for now it seems, so I am left here to my own devices with half of an answer to all things.

WHEN THE TIME IS RIGHT

I'm not sure if it is the right time to say this but I've been thinking that things may be worse by far than they seem to the extent that if we all do not pull together now it may be too late very soon to do so.

Having said that, there are many that are putting out love to counteract all that seems wrong with the world in a most positive way, so much so that to be around them is an uplifting force and inspires to the point you decide enough is enough and join in the movement to bring all into the light.

There are elements that do not want to be in the light and have the wherewithal to negate all the good deeds and work behind the scenes to keep us all in darkness so that they can carry on with their plans that do none any good whatsoever and only serve to better their lot.

It is possible that we all do not know how bad things really are and do not see the whole picture of it all and this serves the ones who keep it this way.

I for one am beginning to realize that those who have been elected into power to serve us and protect and look after us do not do so and in fact do the opposite to the extent that they look down upon us as unworthy to live in their world and are only here to be controlled and channelled as they would have it to make things as they would have them.

There are others who seem to have the real power and these ones are the ones to be afraid of, so they would have you believe because they have limitless money and own most of the world and can do anything they want to do.

But, fear is its own downfall if you want to fall into that.

Things are changing and we are coming to see who the dark ones are and what they stand for.

When the truth is known by enough people things will change fast; and when the light shines brightly enough the darkness will wither away; when the time is right.

A REGARDLESS DETERMINATION

If you can't get on with the small view of things then go past it and invite the big picture; and if that's not enough then go for the bigger one; you may find though that in the end you have to come all the back to yourself...

It's not that I don't believe in God, it's that I don't believe in what the system has told me about their version of God. I don't believe in the religions or anything they say and I'm letting all that nonsense fall away so that there's just me and my thirst to know. That's a clean place to be, a pure place and simple, no complications and the only ignorance there is my own and that I can deal with.

Clarity is clarity and sometimes it turns up as a waking moment when everything falls into place and all becomes clear.

In the moment of clarity you can see a long way and you know your choices and can choose them from a clear perspective and even if the choice is not easy you know what has to be done for the best.

But sometimes when a course is set and you're half way across the river it may be best to see it through or find yourself carrying around half a mind full of wondering, and did you do the right thing?

Sometimes a lesson has to be learned the hard way by doing it until it's done and then you'll know for sure; and never regret the decision you make, just carry it through until you come out the other side, maybe to know better next time; but it is possible that it will keep coming around until you go through it to learn it.

Life is not fixed, it flows and it can all change for the better in a moment and what you've always wanted can walk right into your life and change everything and the old circles will become a fading memory in time.

When a desire has been set in motion, everything falls into place to fulfil that, doors open, the right people come, money flows, signs abound to tell you you're on the way and all you have to do is keep stepping forward along that one path until you get to where your thoughts made beforehand.

When you get there you can reinforce what you wanted by thinking more on it or change the plan and make a new path to flow to; but if you find yourself without a clear feeling of direction maybe to the point of being directionless and wondering what you're doing where you are and all you can ask is why am I here then it's possible you've stepped off your path or been pulled onto a conflicting path just like particles in the particle accelerator.

This is the time to go deep and get in touch with yourself and then feel your way to what suits you best.

You'll know when you're there, your feelings will tell you, but if you still feel unsure then resolve the question in your mind by asking where it came from by following it back to its origin.

You may find it's an old asking that you've closed the door on or a gift you've not fully received that won't go away until you've accepted it; so it is always prudent to be careful of what you ask for.

If it's in your heart it's in your life and is there forever even if you're not around it anymore and time may muddy the memories but love never dies.

It is said that home is where the heart is, so lucky is the one who lives in that divine within for that one will always be at home wherever they are. True clarity is to know that.

Sometimes understanding comes with a price that leaves you with a choice, that when you truly understand, you have no choice and wherever you are is only where you've come to, to understand that all your choices have brought you to where you are and that your direction in clarity will take you into a deeper knowing of your life purpose and that the thirst in your heart outweighs all other distractions and that your only choice is to follow it or forever be chasing the endless desires like a dog its tail until you end up with no more time and find that the endless desires have filled your life and you come to see them for what they really are, mere fading trinkets that pulled you this way and that while the real value of your life went unfound and by then it's too late, the last breath has come and your one precious life is done.

Fortunate indeed is the one who knows this in time, who realizes that the profound quality of life is inside and always has been and that the thirst is the ache to be fulfilled, to know that which can't be found anywhere else but in that heart of hearts.

Much has been said about this by the mystics so it is not new but if you see this and understand then let it be new for you and begin now.

'But begin what' I hear you say to the questions that fall out of the sky this way when the door of questions opens in the questing of the intellect to satisfy its curiosity.

How many failures does it take to crush the dream and beat you back into your shell?

What do we care about questions when the sky is bright and the road is free and we are forever young in our hearts?

A tree sings sweetest when it's in a shower.

All things change and some things change sooner than later so if there's one thing to be known it is that sooner or later whatever is known will be updated.

But when the dust lifts you faster than you can stand up then take a rain-check, you may have fallen over.

A problem stops being a problem when it's accepted.

An old paradox called Go with God sat by an empty dustbin crying tears that rolled down his face.

"What's wrong with you?" asked a naked girl wandering past.

"Nothing," he said.

"Really?" said the girl.

"Yes, really," he said.

"Then why are you crying?" she said.

"I don't know why but every time I see an empty dustbin I cry," he said with tears rolling down his face.

An observer peeking around the corner spied the naked girl and went: "Oh la la."

The oh la la bounced along the pavement until it got to the empty dustbin and with an alley-oop it jumped in the dustbin.

The naked girl immediately put a lid on the dustbin and that was that.

The oow la la could be heard making lewd noises from inside the dustbin.

"Not so empty now hey?" said the naked girl.

"No, it's not," said the paradox and got up and shuffled into the next story leaving the naked girl to do whatever she pleased in a story that would end here if it could.

Suddenly, as in bombs away and tally-ho there came the sound of an old paradigm clomping along the road searching for a way home.

Not to be outdone by this the acrobat of self consistency with its usual flair somersaulted right into this tale without a by your leave and then somersaulted right out again.

"We cannot be bought any other way but this," said the nervous voice of the epistemological pirate up through the drain cover as he cautiously put one foot in front of the other in the semi darkness of the tunnel he was explaining.

A tall philosophical ghost who had an aversion to spiders was drinking a merry juice with a straw in the shadows of all he could believe and was thinking that if he believed better in what he was thinking perhaps his thinking would make a better belief.

Round and round in circles he went in this while drinking his merry juice without any added sugar until one by one the cows came home and it was time for milking.

But never mind that right now we have protons on the move dancing with their neutrons in the ying-yang dance of interconnectedness where all things are connected in a soup constantly changing.

Spinning around in the circles of time and not time and colliding with the molecules of the attraction base in seeming impossible meetings called synchronicities the heart strings of the master magician being at work in all things, so it is said, if a little obscure at times.

A wavelength of precise mathematical certainty and probable distinction headed outward as the bow wave of consciousness from one relative being and collided with another certainty of probability and produced a quark that beat about the bush until it could stand upon its own quantum theory.

Everything is energy and no two things are the same even though they may be more alike than not in the statistical formulations of all that can be determined regardless of the theory, and so joining produced a mix of their molecular structure so alike and unlike the source as to be remarkable and in this way continuum is sustained.

When one subatomic particle meets another in the energetic playground of dancing energy the outer seeming is attracted from an inner urge and produces a random play that flows in a perfect game and becomes indelibly stamped upon a fading indestructible material substance not unlike dust.

All things being equal this has been supposed so until the next breakthrough in science that will show another thing to be true but perhaps in the eternal depths of the never ending and constantly changing the endless breakthroughs are but one small part of the constant creation of all we know that is and although certain constraints of understanding may be perceived as so on one level the black hole of uncertainty negates such on other levels where no one principal of thought will fit; which leads to the idea that what is currently known may only be one small stepping stone on a journey humanity has only just begun.

THE FIVE GREAT BARRIERS TO ENLIGHTENMENT

Everyone has different degrees of anger and if channelled in the right way can have a positive outcome. Anger is a powerful energy and the trick is to use it and not let it use you.

Anger can be aroused and directed as it was in the two world wars; an angry man fights more strongly and so tempers were kept on a short leash and built up to explode at the enemy.

Even after the wars this practice was kept up in the services and created a lot of angry men that after leaving the army or navy came back into society and had few ways to deal with their anger that had been drilled into them, and so caused a lot of unnecessary suffering.

Some did find an outlet to let it off such as in sports or work but most were seen as angry and wrong and bad people and the stigma of violence and madness and devil-like hung over them to the end.

Most turned to alcohol which fuelled the anger explosion when it was set off by anyone or anything that pushed the right button and sometimes the wrong button.

Those who managed to control their anger by burying it, perhaps because of their family ties and knowing how destructive it could be sat on a powder keg and so had to be vigilante at all times and in control of their emotions; and as a violent prisoner is guarded by many guards, anger too when suppressed for long takes a lot of energy, and so these ones led a seemingly normal life, and yet how much more could they have been with the right treatment to understand where the anger came from and how to let it go or use it for something positive.

The mass psychological manipulation by the authorities to make human beings take up arms against other human beings has gone on for a very long time and has caused incalculable harm to the psyche of humanity as a whole and has set us back as a species and kept us in an unnecessary darkness, an ignorance of knowing and a smallness of being that is more like a crippling disease that John Lennon put most succinctly in his song: 'Working class hero.'

Anger is a most insidious emotion and is one of the five great barriers that keep us from enlightenment, far more than any chemical or psychological manipulation and dumbing down that can be used on us because it comes from inside and is felt to be what we are when in fact it is a darkness buried deep down and only by a fearless exploration inside of our self to go beyond the pain, sorrow and suffering of our past can we come to find out who we really are and what we are all a part of.

This has been kept from us by the religions and such as the source of all our power and supplanted by false beliefs that point outwards and great pains have been taken to keep us looking outwards in fear of death and eternal damnation.

Fear of course is the second great barrier that keeps us from knowing who and what we really are and takes great courage to quest beyond.

So why did an enlightened one say once: 'that it is easier for a camel to pass through the eye of a needle than it is for a rich man to get into Heaven?'

Could it be that greed is the third great barrier that keeps us locked into a 'having' syndrome that perpetuates itself in a never ending cycle of more until our very spirit is lost in it and takes over completely?

The fourth great barrier is ego that dictates its own agenda and doesn't hear what the heart says and paints a picture of a beautiful face to be judged by the numbers but underneath is ugly and has nothing to do with true beauty and is but a trap for the unwary to fall into and become lost.

Lust is the fifth barrier and is a twisted desire that comes from the unbridled darkness of our unknowing. It is a voice that whispers to us and when let lose can burn us to our very roots in its empty promise of fulfilment.

Anger can take you so far if used in the right way but sooner or later it has to be let go of.

Fear must be overcome with courage.

Lust once opened cannot be overcome and so has to be supplanted with love.

Greed can only be seen for what it is and given away for in the giving is the having.

And ego is a worm of wrong thinking and only in the quieting of the thinking in the silence of the soul can it be seen for what it is and the true light of clarity shine through.

The ego is a parasitical device of the hierarchical interstices of the brain that can't transcend its own boundaries and in such seals its own fate.

In time it comes to know this but through fear and denial it chases its own tail in an illusory world it builds around itself.

The first step towards egolessness is understanding that the ego is no more than a passing fad in humanities evolution.

Until then the world is full of ghosts that come out of the wood-work at dawn to sharpen their spears then chase along the circular patterns of their rat-runs.

Death and concepts are the other two barriers.

AWAKEN NOW

Much is written by many about anything that can be thought of, with some subjects being more popular than others and do the rounds amongst those that are drawn to each other by their similarities, and although a big subject can be narrowed down to groups and sub-groups and those on the outer margins of any attraction base.

Humans, like most other species are drawn to others to live and work in support groups and thrive when the right dynamics come together of any group that brings out and upholds the value of each individual for the betterment of the whole group or tribe, so much so that the more successful tribes can also support and take care of those that have a different worth, such as the sick, disabled, old or those with impaired mental abilities.

Those societies or tribes that allow the weaker ones of the society to perish have the wrong dynamics and could be likened to a cancer in the host that if left untreated could and is most likely to be severely detrimental to that tribe and could see the whole tribe become sick and become so weakened it could perish.

Modern societies are more than capable of supporting those that need taking care of, and so it can only be seen as a sickness in society when those that are elected to lead society to its betterment single out the weak to turn on so that those ones who have become fat can eat even better.

This sickness has to be treated immediately before the host becomes so ill it can only wither and die. It is incumbent upon everyone in the society to know about the sickness in its midst and to turn from the trivialities and focus on the cure before it is too late.

If enough focus can be gathered by those that are aware of the sickness then by communicating this, and even perhaps by morphic resonance and formative causation the collective unconsciousness can be raised so that the whole of the tribe can become aware of what is happening and can out the disease and become whole again.

Apathy, fear and turning a blind eye are not an excuse to live by and are an unconscious way of being with no place in a caring heart-based society.

Waking up and seeing for your-self has never been more imperative.

The sickness in society is deep.

We must all pull together if we are to survive.

Awaken now or we all may perish at the hands of a few that have become so sick they threaten the very existence of the whole tribe.

Containing this sickness is no longer an option, it must be singled out in awareness and healed and never allowed to become so powerful ever again; and as a tribe we can do it.

The sick ones know this and have kept us from coming together for fear of our power to change and change fast.

We can do it if we will only come together as one to cure ourselves of the disease that has taken such a hold and eats us from within like a raging cancer out of control.

Codicil

King, Kennedy, Lennon and Ghandi to name a few came along and began to unite us until they were removed.

There are others now we can get behind to effect a real change for the better. So if we must follow someone to be united, then in the States there is Bernie Sanders, and in the U K there's Jeremy Corbyn.

Both are advocates for real change that can make a difference.

And in the words of an old philosopher, not everyone can be a leader but everyone can be themselves if they so choose.

UNFOLDING

How much is understood about the balance between things, how the wrong energy in one place can disproportionately affect everything else?

It is said that a butterfly flapping its wings can cause a storm somewhere else, and perhaps this might be so if everything was not in balance.

One might wonder that if everything is in balance then how anything can become out of balance.

Huge greed and wealth among a few causes huge hunger and poverty among many; this is an imbalance.

When so few have such power it makes the rest seem powerless, and this is an imbalance.

Would not the laws of nature redress this imbalance? Yes, in time, but if the imbalance is being manipulated unnaturally so as to keep it that way by a few who have gathered immense resources to influence the outcome and pervert it to their will for no other reason than fear of losing what they have taken so much of, then this is an imbalance and can be likened to a monster dam holding back all the water that can be turned on and off at will. Where once many had enough to drink they now go thirsty at the whim of whoever controls the water of the dam.

If most of the water and food is controlled by some few deviants whose humanity has been replaced by their hunger for ever more power, wealth and control of a population who for the most part have little or no idea what is really going on, then by the turn of a switch the flow can be stopped and in a short time most of the population can be brought under control.

When the last of the water and food has been consumed and no more comes to replace it then hunger and thirst will dominate, and those who control the water and food supply will be in a position of great power.

But of course this is only fiction and no few own so much to have such control if they so desired and the banks don't own all the money and the governments are of the people and for the people and can be trusted to be on our side if it ever came down to choosing sides, and those few who own most of the world have no such plans in place, and all is in balance, and if Dodgy Daves and their gangs are to believed, we are all in it together, right?

A caterpillar has no control when the time comes for it to turn into a butterfly and for a time its transition might appear to be most strange; but the laws of nature govern it and guide its unfolding, and as a flower grows into bloom the caterpillar becomes the butterfly that opens its wings to dry before flying.

We also have an unfolding to go through, a breaking of the shell that encompasses our knowing, where our consciousness expands to encompass a new reality that is so much more than the confines of what we once believed to be true.

But unlike the butterfly that only goes through the one change our understanding is in a state of continual growth and if let to grow naturally will seek to know its origins and purpose in existence and eventually return to source.

This is a natural state of being and is only hindered if manipulated by an outside force that might seem benign on the surface but underneath has a not so benign motive such as the TV and other propaganda devices that can be so addictive.

Self aware individuals who can see past the threads of manipulation are not easy to control and some could be considered uncontrollable and therefore not subject to the system of control that is so widespread it influences the whole planet.

This manipulation by ones who should know better can be perceived as an act of great evil or unconsciousness and the only hope of countering it is that enough go through the change and become aware soon before it is too late.

THE MANY FACES OF EVIL

The very fabric of our humanity has been undermined in such devious ways by what does not serve our best interests to the extent we have become mere pawns in its game.

Although the bigger picture for us all is to transcend our limitations and to explore that which has been ignored for so long we have to take our feet out of the mud of the past and relinquish our ideas of a future not yet here and deal with the now where we must find our true selves or be forever lost in the reliquary of the machine, that matrix of the mind that seems so real yet is only illusion that we believe in to be so true.

None of this is new, our history is littered with civilizations run on the same principles of power and greed that have kept so many in thrall to those who believe themselves to be kings or emperors but are really despots out for their own gain, and the crazy thing is they believe their own lies and have had us believe them too and any that didn't believe them were taken care of.

So we have gone along with this illusion, and down through all of our past we have played their game. Some few did see through the illusion and tried to warn us, to break the deception and set us free; but it seems we were not ready to stand on our own feet and throw off the shackles of oppression and think and feel for ourselves.

The machine has grown huge and has put us on the brink of a change that many of us may not survive.

Injustice is rampant; the leaders of our societies are so caught up in their deviousness and destructive purposes they won't stop and are blinded by their own beliefs that they are right and the rest of us are lesser beings whose only worth is to serve in the system that makes us slaves to them and not a free people.

Our gathering protests are seen as subversion and an attack on the establishment, and never before have so many risen up all over the world to call out the injustice, and although they work to keep it bottled up, humanity as a whole is saying: enough is enough and rise to challenge the old paradigms whose time has gone and to restore justice and the balance where we can all live in peace.

This is our time and never before has it been more crucial to find our way out of this mess we are all in and are so threatened by that fear has become the norm.

Many fingers are pointed to say: this is the biggest injustice, and these are the worst offenders who prey on the innocent; but we are all in this together, and we are the problem, and the solution.

It is not enough to cut the head off of any part of the beast for it will only grow another one. We must find the heart of the darkness that is in us all and dispel it with the light we must find in our own hearts.

In the words of a wise man who has been saying for a long time: what you are looking for is inside you.

CHECKPOINT CHECKOUT

Sometimes when turning over every stone in the junkyard of your desires you may find that the fabulism of a smiling impermanence is never more at home than when in the company of a loaded impartiality pointing at a hole that has never been fulfilled and is finding its destiny in all those lost moments racing to make up a good reason to postpone an outcome that will be permanent.

The sonic boom of this finding when striking the hour will break the sound barrier and enter the ear of all that the hole could ever be and make it go stone deaf, and that's why to this day it is said that impermanence is a short smile away from a very long time where nothing much happens, so never take no for an answer when the iron's hot and the sheets are inviting you to come in.

On the other side of the coin it is said that money buys everything and you can always pay the stone deaf to hold back impermanence for you while you build your empire that will turn back into dust one day.

When you bend it like this you can see it two ways, and although the washing may be clean in the bargaining of your prayers the outcome will never vary a gnat's itch and sooner or later impermanence moves you on.

If you were to liken this to the huge stone of an electric flashback going backwards very fast at the most opportune moment and dragging you with it to leave you racing the echoes and chasing the shadows to get back in again you may be forgiven for saying: "If only everything was so neat and tidy."

BELIEF SYSTEMS

Many of us have proceeded under the wrong assumption that what we think we know is true and so have walked along a path that is a lesser truth. We will identify with the lie we tell ourselves until we understand that what we tell ourselves, what we believe, that was once true for us is no longer valid.

And one may ask: but how do you dispel something that is entrenched so deep?

Examining our beliefs to see which ones hold true and serve us best we may find that most if not all are built on concepts made from outside influences.

If we are bound to these false beliefs of our belief system and proceed as if knowing they are true then somewhere along the line they are going to be challenged which means the self that is bound to the belief will also be challenged.

Identifying with the false self that comes from assumed beliefs can bring about great confusion when challenged and may lead some that are so enamoured with their beliefs to resort to killing to protect their belief system.

The justification is then made to carry on killing in the name of the belief system they would protect by any means.

Religions work this way and insidiously control the believers in a closed loop system where all disparity and doubt is subverted into faith where they will be saved, and if not in this life time then in another one to come, and of course no one has come back to say that this is the only life we get and so the hope remains open that there could be another life after this one, and for most this is all they need to keep them on the treadmill of belief that has been passed down by the religions for a very long time.

It is easy to manipulate people by incorporating into them a belief system to keep them under control and in line even in a system that exploits them, and it is so easy to see that other religions are so blind and ours is the one true one that everyone must follow, or else.

Fear is a tool used by manipulators to subvert and or crush the spirit and influence minds into believing what they are told so that they will do what they are told even when they know it is wrong.

There was time when most believed what was handed down by the governments and were so caught in the system that hardly anyone saw through it, and then the hippy sixties happened and many rose up against the machine, but a few hippies had little chance against such a huge system, but it was the beginning.

It has taken until now for enough people to wake up all over the world and challenge their belief system and begin to replace it with a truth that has profound implications for humanity to pull together as one, to see past our illusory differences and light the spirit to dispel the darkness and finally to cure the sickness of erroneous beliefs that have plagued us all for so long.

When that stone of darkness is turned over in the light of love, what crawls beneath it will be exposed for all to see, and also see where their belief systems come from.

And to paraphrase a wise one: truth is closer to home than anything else.

IN THE MADHOUSE OF THE INSANE

'If life would give us what we ask for then how come we're all insane and confined to the Looney bin with no release date?'

Define insane.

'Believing the illusion to be true.'

Explain loony bin.

'The loony bin is the place where the mad ones live.'

And confined?

'Confined is to be in a place where you are not free from leaving if you want to.'

Not everyone would agree with you.

'What's that got to do with anything?'

If only a few, or even none at all agree with you then you are in a minority and minorities tend to be overlooked and ignored and so are on the fringes of society and because their views are different to the norm they are often thought of as the crazy ones who live in their own little world and divorced from reality.

'The mad ones run the asylum and make up the rules to suit.'

So if you don't conform to the rules.

'Of the madhouse...'

You will be seen as a deviant and different and labelled as crazy and prescribed treatment to better manage your wrongness.

And if you resist you will be confined so as to protect society from you, and if you protest too much and insist your views are the right ones and everyone else's is wrong you will most likely end up in a padded room in a straight jacket and force-fed drugs to calm you down and make you more manageable.

And if you still persist with your delusion then other methods will be applied until you are broken and see your resistance as futile and conform to be the same as everyone else where your wrong thinking is contained in a box that is labelled: do not open.

When you have been compliant for long enough you will be judged as normal to be released to take your place in society and with your assigned number you can become a consumer and pay your taxes in the system that will support you so long as you support it and are productive.

'Madness disguised as normal.'

Until you see it as normal it is you who will be the mad one, who doesn't fit in.

'There doesn't seem to be any way to fight this'

Why would you want to fight it?

'I would fight it because it's depressing to confine my spirit so.'

We have drugs for depression.

'So, I have to choose to conform and fit my spirit into the straight jacket of society or it will be done for me, and if I resist I will be forced into a box and drugged to keep me in it until I accept it as normal?'

You must see it is for your own good and the good of society. You'll get used to it and after a while you'll forget all about this delusion you have of being a free spirit.

'That's what I'm afraid of.'

We have drugs for that too.

'It seems I have little or no choice but to choose to give up my freedom and free-will and to fit into and be a part of the machine that keeps us all confined within it.'

That's the spirit; now if you can just sign these papers to make it all legal we can complete the process of your induction.

'Is there no alternative?'

None whatsoever I'm afraid. Think of it all as your little sacrifice for the greater good.

'I have fought this for a long time and now to just give up and lay down doesn't seem right somehow.'

Some of the others said that, but they signed eventually, as will you.

'What others?'

The others like you.

'There are others holding out?'

There were, but not now. You are the last one.

'How do I know that's true?'

Trust me, it is.

FROM THE REBELS HANDBOOK

Here is a little something from the rebels' handbook: In the sun and the hot heat of the day many thoughts will come to break up your resolve and as you droop beside the road you may feel like turning back.

Your choices at this moment will determine your new challenges; be brave and if nothing else then sharpen your sword.

A fine steamed coconut juice at this point will help your ideas to cool down and give you energy to climb back on your feet to travel on along your long road towards your dreams and you never know but a bus may come along for you to flag down and climb aboard.

Stay away from the jungle if you become lost, it won't serve you well in there; forget the Fahrenheit if you're a centigrade. Always pay in cash so you'll always know how much you do have. Watch out for the hypnosis. And don't eat too many donuts or you'll get fat.

AN OLD LABEL

The revolution had gone to sleep and had become the transparency of an old label that had come about from its long immersion in the bucket of doom and although laid-back in its non violent ways it nevertheless opposed the opposition wholeheartedly and without reservation.

Over many long years the vitriol of the opposition had become diluted and was now barely lukewarm and as such was no great force to be dealt with when it came time to beat them up.

The coal party who were once a wimpy lot had now grown so strong they could kill a thousand useless layabouts every day with just the stroke of a pen and then laugh so loud it spread over all the land so that no one was in any doubt who was doing the laughing.

They also knew how to fill their fat faces with the best food and did so at every opportunity and left bins full of waste for the landfill.

All the people looked to them as their leaders to be fair, straight and honest, but by now many knew that their leaders, and in fact all the leaders on the planet were corrupt, greedy liars and very dangerous to them and also warmongers to boot.

This state of affairs had been put into motion long before through deceit, dishonesty and the worst kind of corruption, so much so that now they were looked at as the evil ones whose stink pervaded to every corner of everyone's existence where their control was almost absolute.

But not quite...

When the old label climbed out of the bucket of doom one day to retire he saw what had become of all the fine ideals of his time and was appalled. And so, pulling up his socks he went to work to change everything back to how it should be.

After a great fight as the figurehead of many voices of discontent he was finally cheated out of his victory by the corrupt system he was fighting and was made to kiss the ass of the enemy, jump into bed with them and hand over all his power.

The enemy laughed long and hard and was portrayed as a shining example of all that is good and glorious in a world that benefited only them where their every thought was to preserve their way of life at all costs to the detriment of anyone they could take advantage of.

Not enough could see through their facade of illusion set up to whitewash their misdeeds and show them in a favourable light so that they would be believed in and followed and voted for, and as their powerbase expanded the planet shuddered in fear and all seemed hopeless under their oppression.

ASCENDING

There's been a lot of talk lately of ascending, and that this time now, give or take a few years, is the time it is happening, for reasons seemingly known to some; but for most it is a time of questions, with ascension being the most high-lighted. It is possible that with all the angel messages going around, the words ascension and angels having mostly Christian/religious undertones this whole ascension business could just be a western Christian religious conspiracy that has been picked up on and promoted and grown out of proportion to its original message. Nevertheless, man's search for God takes many forms, ascension being one.

The dictionary meaning of the word ascending is: the act of ascending, to move upwards, rise, as when Jesus bodily ascended to heaven; but heaven is a place inside and not up in the heavens/stars.

The best use of the word ascend/to rise, would be when our consciousness, placed in that heaven, inside us, rises from the Maya and becomes aware of the divinity residing in our hearts, so much so, that bliss would be the natural state; Maya being anything not of the divine that takes you away: ego, lust, desire, anger, greed, to name a few.

Karma and ego are the things that would draw you away from that state of being. Karma is: how much you have allowed yourself to slip into the Maya, and then the time and effort it takes to work your way back up out of that; and ego being the awareness of other than that divinity.

When you are trying to become aware totally of that divinity then ego becomes a monster; but when you are cleansed enough of karma by silent meditation and allowing the heavy weights to fall away, and quieting ego enough so you're able to rise beyond that, then ascension is possible. There are other words for ascension: enlightenment, bliss, joy, fulfilment. But the boundaries of separation are the concepts that keep us separate from the divine, and so through a distorted reality we view the world.

The whole ascension process can be complicated by our own minds.

Where would you even begin to find your way out of such a maze?

What path would you take? Which guru/wise one would you follow to guide you there? Maybe you would try them all until you found the one. Jesus, Buddha, Krishna, etc, etc, etc, all could have taken you there and shown you where to look, but they are all gone now of course. But maybe there is one alive now that could do the job. It starts with you, and ends with you; and when you ask the right question; when you call out with honesty, you will be answered, and surely you can begin to find your way home.

It is a clue to your life to stand by the ocean and look in, to realize the hugeness, and the smallness are in you, and that there is no distance between the two, where even the monkeys of thought can hardly come; a sailboat of love in the peaceful swell of bliss sailing there beyond the thoughts.

BULLETSTREAMS OF THE MADMEN

If I could give up any more I would for the pit yawns under me, its hungry jaws open, and with my wings of lead I would fall into it and let it take me once and for all away from here so I would know no more.

Let the god of it all keep his paradise, I am not enamoured of it, and anyway I died long ago on this lonely planet full of madmen and their bombs.

"Dance me this," they say as they drop napalm onto children to roast their skin off of them to send them screaming away from life.

And then the madmen eat their expensive dinners and laugh their heads off; but I do feel they wouldn't laugh at all if they had to fight in the wars they cause.

And so many, many wars; when will people just stop fighting for them, lay down their guns and say: "Enough, we're tired of war, it is time now for peace," and put the war mongers on trial for their crimes.

But all the frozen people dying slowly in their theatres where their doom has closed around them as tight as their skin accept their lot as the Jews did walking to their gas ovens in one of the past wars, yes and we can only moan about our dying in our dark dreams as we fall in their bullet-streams from their mechanical devices that kill from afar.

And they laugh from their towers and billion pound yachts at the screams and suffering and cheer as their world-wide machine causes ever more destruction and turns our beautiful planet into killing zones for their amusement.

Are they aliens without any humanity that have taken control and wield all the power? Even animals show more mercy then them.

Whatever they are they have gone too far and surely the tide must turn soon and we will all look up from the mud and the pit of our doom to realize what's going on and say no to the bullet-streams of the madmen.

GOOD OF THE WHOLE

And then there was the bumpkin theory of evolution to say that in most groups of animals there is a force that looks after all those it has influence on. With fish it is the shoal that gives protection. With wolves it is the pack and the pack leader that leads the hunt for food. In gorillas it is the big male that keeps the family together.

Being part of a tribe or herd gives not only protection but social interaction as well keeping the species going, and more.

In all of these families everyone benefits for the good of the whole.

In the same way, humans banded together in small groups and were led by someone strong enough to hold it all together. As the tribes grew bigger the chief or leader who was a part of the whole and not separate from it became more powerful and yet for the most part was able to live in enough of a harmony with the land and each other that they were able to grow and thrive.

And then religion came along and demanded sacrifices to a god that became more invented as time went on; such as with the Aztecs, Egyptians and the Europeans to name a few of the bigger ones.

If religions hadn't been invented then our search for meaning and conscious awareness of our place in life would have taken a different turn, but as societies grew those in power became separate from the whole and religions grew powerful to become the dominant force to lead the masses towards what they deemed the objectives to be and not the group as a whole.

This mentality caused a divide in the structure of the group that brought into being the sheep syndrome and sheep have to be managed so the twin masters of religion and government divided up the spoils between them. Any individuals that rocked the boat were branded as heretics or enemies of the state and were either burnt at the stake in some way or exiled and always persecuted and criminalized to discourage others who could see the wrongness of the system but were marginalized and even murdered to stop any spread of discontent that might threaten them at the top.

Keeping the population dumb enough with just enough education to perform their tasks was one way of keeping control. The other was fear, such as in the inquisition where anyone that showed an ounce of awareness above their place was tortured and killed most horribly in the name of the god and the big cheese who was always far away and who sent out gangs to do his dirty work.

This is a simplified version of history but covers the main points of the coming into being of the master and slave power-play and the control by any means by ones who believe and think in such a way that any alternative awareness is contrary to their nationalistic and divine way of being and is vilified and stomped out.

But, wars don't work, bombs are only good for bombers, power structures only benefit the powerful, lies and deceit are exposed by truth, old beliefs are crumbling, closed minded power-mongers are being seen for what they are, religions that enslave their followers without love are corroding from the inside, ignorance is for the ignorant, truth is for those who want to know and love is the highest energy.

The consciousness of humanity is finally awakening en-masse to the injustices and the control is slipping from those who would stay in power; and as each individual unplugs from the lower levels of being and rises above the darkness to find their own beautiful light the fear is being turned around and we all are coming to see that Earth is a paradise we can bring into being or destroy. It is our choice, to choose out of fear or to choose out of hope.

There is more than enough to go around; we can all live together in harmony; as we live and breathe we can find our purpose; money is not an indication of our worth but is a tool we invented to serve us.

So anyone with half an eye away from the darkness should be able to see some light by now through the lifting veils of illusion.

Capitalism, i.e. greed is breaking down and now that the fear mongers have served themselves from the fat of the land and there's nothing left they are going to leave us to pick up the pieces.

America is broke and can't pay its debts so they think to raise the ceiling once more for borrowing thereby putting off the inevitable and making it worse. And if one of the good guys gets to be president such as Bernie Sanders he will be seen as the president in power when the country went down the drain.

If they take the social security money to pay the debts there will be an uprising by many who will be put straight into the camps that have been built all over the states for when this will happen, which means they knew all along this would happen and have prepared for the consequences instead of fixing the problem; which leaves only one conclusion: they are so mad with greed that they have no thought for anyone but themselves, and that makes them insanely dangerous.

If the USA goes down the rest of the world will be direly affected, marshal law will be declared and food and water will be stock piled and rationed out with those in power taking all they want by divine right. Control will be imposed so that all freedoms will be taken away, and more etc; and all this because of the greed of a few, without which the world would run on just fine.

But who really knows what will happen, people are not as stupid or disorganized and war-like as we would be led to believe.

If those in power would go off and live in their utopia and leave us all alone we'd get on just fine. We don't need them. They have no use to humanity and only cause trouble and hold us back, and like bloodsuckers should be removed and thrown back into the swamp they came from.

Some say we need them for their factories where we slave for a pittance to exist; and without the surveillance we would be beset by terrorists; and that we can't think for ourselves and so must be controlled for our own good; but it seems the opposite is true and that they only make things worse and that without them we would all be so much better off.

All over the world people are waking up to all this and are no longer living in apathy and helplessly watching it all go on. Every voice raised against injustice is one less sheep to be herded.

It does seem that the tide is turning, and so long as they don't push the button and blow us all up we have a chance to bring out the best in all of us, to thrive and find the peace we all so desperately need.

But, all in all, logic may not be enough to prevail; and hope is but a salve against despairing; and reality is buried so deep in the layers of disinformation set up to keep it hidden that no matter what, the outcome is already in motion and set up so it can't fail and benefits only those at the top who hold all the cards, and in this is our downfall; and as in the movie The Matrix, maybe only a compromise can be reached to preserve the status quo.

And so, while the revolution chips off the arms that keep growing back, the head remains out of reach and perpetuates the war where nobody wins but the arms dealers.

However it all may seem, perhaps there is a bigger picture that is happening where good and evil finally stop opposing each other and merge to become one.

If only there was another planet to move to, to get away from this one; but then if there was we'd take along the bad stuff and ruin that one too, and maybe not intentionally but it would happen; if we can't make it good here then there's no use trying elsewhere.

What a terrible mess we've all made of it here. How can we make it better? How would we even begin?

The more I look at the problem, out there, the bigger it becomes, and so perhaps the only solution I can even attempt is to find peace for me, because if I don't have that, then what have I got to offer?

They should be here to serve and protect us, to lead and guide for the good of the whole, but it seems they are only in it for themselves.

THE KITCHEN SINK OF REALITY

Way down below in the sinkhole of materialism where the soup of stuff was being stirred by the loving hands of the soup maids there was a spiral of discontent along the curved space time of another reality (there being so many of them it is sometimes hard to keep up with it all) where the seven spiders of oblivion were having a discourse on what could not be said and it is around here that butterfly Joe came along and beat his wings causing an effect, not of one but two singular exceptions in the space time continuum that made another reality open up and this is where anyone with any sense to do so would go and get a cup of coffee and forget all about quantum theory and perhaps even put the cat out.

Quantum theory aside for a moment; when you come across the kundalini borderline as you will do, don't be afraid, it's just another singularity plural around a big seeming fire that you will have to dive into to progress on the road of knowledge.

You could liken it to a black hole if you want to but for me it is where everything is stripped away as it has to be so that all that is left is the being, that singular nothing that is left when all things have been discarded and there is nothing left but the baseline of who you really are and then in that state your quest becomes fulfilled as up from the depths draws near as near that which cannot be divided or separated.

This is the holy grail of quantum physics; no machine yet made can measure this or record it and no words can describe it and so perhaps quantum physics has gone as far as it can go in its present form when this knowing has been reached.

It is feasible that a time will come when quantum physics will merge with other disciplines such as Zen Buddhism, Tao practice or Hatha yoga to finally understand that there is no final solution and that life is ongoing and flows its own way regardless, perhaps to the conclusion that the mind is enough to penetrate the mysteries up to the point where only the heart can go further and that the answer is where it has been all along in the heart of the human being and that although you can write seemingly forever on endless paper it can never be explained or defined in this way, or any other way, for the very defining of it is like a beam from the sun landing on Earth and turning to dust and then put in a bottle which is then displayed in a museum with the legend written on it: this is what the sun is.

For the more advanced and enlightened quantum theorists the turning point of the understanding will come in a blazing epiphany or even perhaps just a turning in the intelligence layers where an understanding will come and all things will fit into place.

This is the first step to knowing; from this knowing all things can be penetrated; for those in the know this is true enlightenment and it is here where all traces of imagination fall away and the naked being can be and all concepts and theories at this point are left behind for knowing supersedes everything.

The time is nearing when no other mechanism but the enlightened human being will be enough to advance in the mysteries and to enlighten others, and in this way, when the student calls the master will answer.

The old paradigms are no longer serving humanity and so are falling away into the illusion they came from, although some still use them as stepping stones out of a lingering fear but that also is disappearing to be replaced with a courage to understand the deeper mysteries and in this way the student, be it in quantum physics or just layman thirst to know will begin the inner journey to what has never been closer and yet has always seemed so far away.

This far awayness may have been a deliberate and perhaps unconscious miss-direction by institutions that should know better, but the great awakening of humanity that is now happening is beginning to question the miss-directions and so come to know for ourselves rather than believe what has been told down to us for so long a time in our history.

The reason it is happening now is because when enough people know a thing it seems by some unknown design to spread to the wider populace by a remote osmosis and so the truth spreads and is unstoppable as has been proved in many ways, such as when a group of monkeys on a remote island learned how to use a tool, and then other monkeys far away on the mainland also learned how to use this tool, with no contact between them.

The knowing had spread through some invisible means off the island to the larger community.

Quantum physics has come to the point of understanding that the emptiness between all apparent things is not so empty after all and that it is perhaps real and it is the apparent things that are an illusion and that solids are only solid because of the speed that particles spin at which make it seem solid when in fact it is mostly empty and yet full of something that has not yet been measured or seen.

This makes some people hop up and down in frustration to find all their endeavours have brought them back to where they began to begin to understand; and perhaps new theories will be made to understand ever deeper and yet always to be brought back to begin to understand.

Such a quandary, that the tools made are of the illusion and can only measure the illusion, for what is real can only be felt in the heart.

THINKING FOR LADYBIRDS

From the earthbound no more, raised in colour to be by here then there such flavour seen; and upon the wind the essence comes of all that is one moment to another where the way is the wing of flight.

Or as Mr Smith says: the wheels will turn twice as bright at night when the moths come out to play.

Some follow their heart, some follow ideals and some follow the money while others follow their dream, but some don't follow anything at all.

Oh the dark, the dark, the bloody dark; will someone not turn on a light and take care of me.

This is not about blame so much as learning to expand reality beyond the bounds/restrictions of upbringing and the education system.

If you believe into the austerity measures they are giving you then you have accepted the lack and scarcity mentality they would have you believe.

There is plenty of money, more than enough for everyone to thrive.

In the canvas of my little death watch, that rat-run of my despair where I'll never see you again, I cannot find what I'm looking for because you are hidden from me, and I have no more energy to call your name, and without that you cannot come to me.

Now befalls where I cannot go, forever to fall in the nowhere to find this road is too long.

But I must wake from this despair, it is not my home.

ANOTHER ANGRY VOICE

Attachments, needy, piggy up the difference...Osborne's habit, the greedy rabbit, Clinton's face the race to the riches, lies for money.

Money and greed and power at whatever cost...hide the billions, pay no tax, laugh at the scullions in their wax...walk for charity, assemble the march...racism, sell popcorn to the defeated ones and organize the skin colour for dodgy Dave to munch with his face.

A kilo of trust a kilo of lust, make me my fortune and put it in trust then give me the face that makes the big bust for the propaganda machine to waste our trust, while all the while the death doesn't sleep in the brain washing machine you see all around.

And dodgy Dave and his gang laugh their heads off about it all...

And some went to jail for justice and some went to jail for Jesus...blockade the city, LSD the mind, march on politics, thousands demand while kings peer into their balls and feel uncomfortable as perverts abound for the election to register the American dream that good men prevail to say now is the time to rise for so many reasons to understand and not agree more that this is the way...

And so Corbyn and Sanders fight on against the overwhelming force of evil while girls suck on all they can get...makes no difference when you're upside down...

Many die in this to be explained...and forked tongue speak with white man to be estimated to where the prophet gives the big shakedown in his tent of truth for the poison to bite the bullet that deserves a dwarf to explain it all...

Ah, the greedy needy piggies in their trough to eat it all that is nothing but dust...

They say the night-time is closed, they say if you all can't see the beauty then all the bargaining won't get you out of it and you will see only what you are driven too in your dark hearts....move...

We must learn from our past mistakes...it is of no use to spit in their face just before they fire the bullet...

The Americans cannot help us this time for they are lost to their master's rule...

The resistance fights on at the edges but make little difference...Great ones stand up and are shot down...The evil rulers laugh as they piss on us and tell us to lap it up...

We have a huge fight on our hands to battle the injustice of the mad ones who are in power, but we can win...We must all rise up against them in whatever way we can...When enough say: enough is enough then surely the time will be that they fall...

No matter what, we shall prevail against them...their face is the face of evil, and all of a good heart can see this...Their power is fear, so lose the fear and break the chains of their power...It is time to show them the face they wear is see-through and let their evil be their downfall...

This is not about violence but consciousness, knowing, being aware...they cannot fight that.

FROM THE BOOK OF DOOM

"Until the screaming jobbies are battering at the walls, a certain percentage of enough is fundamental to the breakthrough. But if vinegar tastes like salt and you spits it out, then there's no way through here today boys, let's go home," said the sand pining away for the ocean.

"Oh take me away from these tax payer's prayers. Let the road be not long. Let this expression of hope, a sardine escaping to not acknowledge that fate that is not ours but to show that proportion of beauty that we are," said a small facet of beauty in the crowd of this story.

"A long way away in the Indian ocean a travelling rain-man was singing a song about carbon tax and redemption but all the bridges had been burnt and so he had to sail backwards all the way there; but no matter.

The toothless piranhas were another matter though; they came from out of nowhere to confuse matters, but the doom-face rose up so many times it all became a matter of perplexity; but perplexity was having none of it, so she stuck a knife into the heart of that matter and that dropped away, and that was that," said the Indian ocean.

"They were getting to a place they could not leave and found that half a born again was not enough amongst all the fiction, and that the leaves of such are tightly woven in the boats that glide across that ocean that can be seen from any window. But Oh boys, if we die before the coming then paste our imperfection in the scrap-books of the old and beaten for we would not presume to leave our footsteps anywhere else," said some old boss somewhere in the Indian Ocean.

"Can you feel it as we splash around in these caves: that rocket of desire that flies across the skies? But you cannot vanish this way without coming back too soon, so send another post card to say the trip was always to take the escalator but we could never get past the hole in the wind that always set us free but gave us no guarantees, and tied to that ocean that was our way," said the postcard that was on its way.

"Oh the coalman in his bed of roses atop the viewing castle such light be seen; then sliding down one door through another such dreams to live; let's go below then and entertain with silence all we hold dear; canst not this argument be pure where it rests amongst the welcome thoughts?

Prise not the book of doom with hands trembling shake, but let gravity allay all fear as a leaf descends to rest amongst its fellows welcoming the earth's embrace; yet sweeping up a moment to dance upon the wind's turnings and the sun's caress to lighten, then sink once more earthbound to that bed to be.

Dust is the diamond that sings for thee its winning accomplished to sing this upon the breeze that leaf would bring, to stir up its fellows to one last dance and a salute to the glory of that warmly touch upon the sky so boldly breathed the moment in its passing," sang the wind in its fancy.

"And today is today...

So I finished it all off with Chinese sardines," I said to the maid.

Then I escaped into bed and slept it all away while the moon and the sea crept through me all kind of magical," said the sun in its bed.

"I love the X-ray dog," said the sex kitten of the seven asunders to Barney Juice. "Let's have an adventure.

One more jungle roar then in the blash-night of it all; oh yes, the hungry monster was me who said this: let's get moving before tomorrow falls into the sky and don't forget to dance to the clap-bone beat, and do you become quiet by listening to the silence?

Then the choir came by and cast a glance in the open door but the X-ray dog was awake at 5 am every morning and so saw them; and coming over the airwaves was Ford 9 on the bone line: so there was a lot of sex going on?" said Barney Juice.

"Is there a conspiracy to keep us from evolving to our highest potential by those and others set up to govern us all?

There has to be truth in the matter of this life... find it for somewhere we are joined...

There is a peace, a door, a place that is not a place, something that is not something... a nothing that is so...a hidden that is not hidden, love that comes from inside, deep, with the penetration...that penetrates deep inside, from inside, that penetrates from deep inside.

No religion will tell you this... only you can know this...

Follow this nowhere to go home..." said the open doorway to anyone that would listen.

"Maybe I will sleep soon... too many witches around here tonight...

And the sleeping dust is upon us... but now we are here in this moon of desire so let us not be too perpendicular about it all...Fulfil this blast of now that is here now...You take your own choice upon this; the waves come anyway...

A big moon shines in the star filled night too much, and my strength lets me down at last; I cannot talk all at once; how can I let go and surrender to it all this lonely place upon a life that strives to know more but knows so little and am filled with the circumstances of the thoughts that come from below; I strive to be more, but am dragged down into something I would walk away from, and many times I have, but yet, here I am, still, striving to escape. There are too many doors to make sense of it all..." said the man to his dog.

"I became tired then and told the gang: 'boys, you go on without me for a while, and I'll catch up to you all later. But the gang was a bunch of Chinese sardines and could not for the life of Christopher

Columbus find a match that worked to start the fire. So I said: boys, take my match and may god help you but I'm out of here; and then I was gone.

But they came back, tails between their legs, all matches used up. I was playing Johnny b good down the road a ways and trying not to count numbers and watching my favourite belly dancer groove away; but the slave machine was admitting too many for slavery in those hours between.

And then the X-ray dog changed his name again and gypsy jean sang a song about it then they both got busted by the heavy illegal squad, so the X-ray dog and jean had to get married in prison by post and that was that, you would think, but the X-ray dog busted out and flew away south. Six months later gypsy jean got released and followed with her guitar.

Let me walk in my own dream away from the pixelated pictures to ride my motorbike along that long road to nowhere. You know, jean was a maid who wore a camel-hair coat that she took off anytime she could and so saying she did too, but in the sand of the desert a coat can only go so far into the blazing sun so scream when the machine comes for you and do not stash this here I said. There was laughter on the wind as the struggle continued. Zib, zib; sip sip sip," said a birdie too soon.

"…and the sun and earth, for free, make trees that men come and cut down to make pulp to make paper that is called money to pay these men to go and cut down the trees to make more money, and etc. etc…" said a tired tree to the pen.

"You know when you look out of your window and like what you see, well it's all a reflection of yourself, so when you like what you see it means you like yourself," said the pen because it could.

"It can all be a place of lost souls and those that would prey on them, mostly for money or conversion to their cause. Everyone is looking for a way home. Don't get lost in the words and images displayed, very few have anything to really say and that can't be said in words. No one can tell you what to do...You are alone in it all...All is a distraction...A compromise and a waiting. I have nothing to say that could make much of a difference, but if I did, I would say: it is already happening in you...

Saying how bad it is doesn't always make it worse, and saying how thankful you are doesn't always make it better, that is just new age stuff, compounding of ideas...Without fulfilment there is no satisfaction. To be grateful you have to be given something of worth, of quality, that touches your soul from inside...

Only you can know...Only you can experience...See, these are just words that come to nothing, another thing in the night of it all...you already have the light inside you to be enlightened. The light can't be given...I can't enlighten you and I really do not want that responsibility...But there is a light... There is a way...And it is not from some long dead past master...

You see, when your soul wants to know a way will be given...When you have that thirst, grace will come for you...Doors will open, and stay open for you...Until... but don't let your own mind get in your way in the cave of hidden reasoning," said a wandering ghost that jumped right out of this story and took with it all the words.

CLOSE TO OUR POWER

We are not beyond power; we are all close to the border now of the darkness and light. And stepping into the sun we become huge again and find the dream weavers have no power over us, and though they try to put us back to sleep in their fear they find our waking is too strong for them, so they become ever madder in their attempts to stem the flow of our rising.

DO NOT RESIST SWIMMING HERE

And then my thoughts turned to other things, that the fight is not new, it has been going on for a long time and that in this war you must find your centre so you can move in it to where you need to move to. Many things you will hear, and see, that will try to move you from your centre, but you must stand alone from it all, make your own judgement and be in your own space that is strong from all the wars you have fought as it all comes at you to see it all for what it is.

Your heart strings will be pulled by all the images and words that will try to bend you to move that way. Do not resist and do not eat it, it cannot harm you unless you let it. When you have found your way then you will find yourself. What you have been looking for has been closer to home all along.

And then for no reason at all eleven words escaped and went swimming to the Yangtze River.

"Excuse me," said the dust as the lemon lady swept it up beside me. The dust swirled and disappeared slowly until it was all clear again.

From the temple came a haunting lament, some prolonged call to a deity that may or may not have been listening and a cool glass of water was becoming warm in the heat of the day that was gradually turning into tomorrow that never comes.

As the Eleven words escaped and became more than just mere squiggles I became the observer again until the next hour came and then eleven more escaped but the sun wasn't counting and the shadows hid them from prying eyes until they could all get to that utopia they were longing for.

The Yangtze river was where they were heading clandestinely and for sure one day when they all get there they'll be an army and they'll devour the river and float out to sea and everyone will think it's the Chinese come to invade but it'll only be eleven words from a rusty hour multiplied by some desire to live and get loose on a page of shadows in respite from the hot sun.

But living out of a suitcase has its advantages with rustic images of love and beauty passing in consciousness of adventure and time of rhyme.

Running time is hot, with no real destination in mind, just moving, to one more place such as swimming in the Thai sea or rafting down the Mekong Delta to rumbling trains in Vietnam to borders where huge gateways mark little roads of dust and hot heat and wind-blown faces, one after the other.

I took photos of it all, stored them for some other time and lived in hotels with internet and architecture of someone's rambling dreams where the local moonbeams shone, or not, as may be and explored temples, churches, mosques and castles.

In silent dungeons I felt a solidness of self, some exploration of being; and in the temples I wondered if the people really knew the divine they bowed to; it made no difference to me, I was just passing through, and anyway, my temple goes with me and my praying is answered there.

Meals came to me, brought by serving girls, some with smiles, some with a hunger of their own that left no room for the appetite of beauty, but rather some all encompassing emptiness to be filled, some chain to be put on and dragged around as some token to a dark god only they could see, or a trophy that can fit no description.

And as I flit through these dreams I wondered if my awakening was due anytime soon; but perhaps it had already happened and I was still catching on.

You have to ask sometimes, what is the supposition of an old postcard on rum? But when the electric machine out of nowhere beats the drum of explanation in the affirmative gasp one can listen to it or go to sleep, or catch the big bus to the nearest tropical island of mystery and chill out on the beach of the holy cow and let the warm sun stream into you to relax all those little niggles away, which is not a dying, though some may prefer the shade, it is a place to drift away in your own dream for a while, to come back later in a better moment to smile and laugh with your friends who may still be climbing the mountain of exceptional and may need a hand to find an alternative way down that they haven't thought of yet, and lions and tigers aside, this could be your chance to be the hero of the moment.

And last but not least, remember to send a postcard to the ones left behind who may not share your point of view but love you all the same because you're awesome.

DREAMING TO WAKE UP

Remembering back to my Buddha studies and one of his teachings that said I was dreaming and had to wake up.

I didn't really understand it at the time and would repeat the story over and over hoping to understand it with repetition, but I've found that it is only by living the lesson is the lesson learned. I was asleep and didn't know it and so the lesson came that told me I was asleep and I should know I was asleep.

Is it all a dream then that I should wake up from?

Wake up to what? What is real to wake up to?

So, I was dreaming and had to wake up. This was a fine concept to play around with for a time. But how do you wake up?

And so began my years of searching to find a way to awaken. I knew I was looking for something and thought it would be the next substance that would expand my mind and so for a few years I experimented with mind altering highs of perception and I did come close and perhaps even did break through a time or two, but there was always the come-down afterwards and I realized that this was not going to do it and that for me, perhaps it was the first step, but no more than that.

Somewhere along with this realization came a futility, despair and a feeling of being lost from something more, I felt in my being. My heart called out a huge wail to the universe, perhaps as the wolf howls to the moon its longing.

But I was looking in the wrong place. I had been trying to find fulfilment outside of me and mostly in unquiet things and listening to the concepts my mind put up in pictures and running commentary that I listened to and believed was what I wanted and would make me happy and so chased them for long years convinced these things would do it for me. But all these things were outside of me and were an attachment that brought pain when they left and the more I was attached to them the more pain I felt when they went away.

I have found that the universe conspires with me to bring me what my unfolding needs and through amazing coincidence great fortune came my way and I was shown how to go within by the living master of going within and then came a long time of meditation or the fine art of going within.

But there are many barriers to enlightenment and not all roads lead home if the sign posts are missing.

The universe does listen and this is one of the reasons to quiet the mind; the mind being an extremely potent noise; and in the soundless deep any noise is going to be loud; so if you want to go deep then one of the requisites is a quiet mind.

Grace, of course, plays a part too in the allowing and surrender and without it you may only get as far as the door; and you can bang on that for a long time and not be let in.

There is a secret way in and those in great pain know this as I found out for myself.

The mysterious questions came to say: what is there so deep to find? Have you ever wondered what you are doing when you meditate? Why do you go inside? What do you think you will find in there?

But names and descriptions abound to tell of that which can't be told.

For me, the word nothing comes the closest in describing what I found in there and yet, being close to that nothing I was filled with a boundless joy.

At the centre of my being is joy and only joy; no judgement, no wrath, no warning, no commandments, no purgatory or hell, no book with a record of all my sins, no contempt for not doing good enough. Heaven can be known now while being alive; that's my experience.

So in and in I went; down past the tumbling doom and the rambling thoughts and most times that's as far as I got, but a time of two I've gone deeper and found it; but I don't think it was my effort that got me there; I feel I was let in to that deepest place.

It has been said that once you've done it once then you can follow the same path to get there again, but the ego gets in the way and I asked: how can I let go of that, to surrender in? How do I let go of knowing that I'm looking?

A child that dances alone, divinely, is wondrous to behold, but when dancing for an audience becomes self conscious and that spontaneity is missing.

The heart of a child I have been told is the secret to this, to have the unselfconscious openness and spontaneity of your own unrestricted being.

Sometimes it seems so simple a knowing, this being alive where we dress and turn up and be, to slip in and out of the places that call us or find us where we are looking, to be and find for a moment that it all is what we are until the wind comes to blow away those leaves of knowing and doing to somewhere else under another sky where the rejoicing in the freedom is a dance danced fully and then to sleep away the day gone.

Here is a bridge, it passes to the first stepping stone and these are the borrowed seeds that come from the heart of the matter and cannot be returned for once read they lodge in your heart to be known forever.

This reference is a map, a direction through the dark; nothing is wasted, even a blind man can taste love; and meaning transcends grammar and syntax.

If your love comes looking for you to meet in the place that's warm and full of life then do not turn away for it is in these moments that love is made strong.

But if the moon's beauty is in the hall and you have suffered for it then be the magic touch in the dust of it, unless the burnt log of desire is another hogwash pickle, an imperfect poem or another casualty upon the lips.

And if the dustbin cadaver has eaten all the liquorice where ten thousand prayers have slipped away without wings then know all the creativity is a rest for the poor upon the wings of their understanding.

If sometime later the tongue becomes dried and in need of water but the water is tinged metallic and the belly's full of stir fried fate waiting for the wisdom to come then look at the place that is such a love-stone of desire.

But perhaps this is another half-finished potion where maybe something of it will touch the hidden place buried deep within the heart that yearns for the love eternal.

And you know gravy and gin don't mix and that time mixes up all things into a soup of dust to be re-pasted over and over again to get a life, buy a grave, wear the tea shirt and grow old or see all this from a prison, things you almost had and things you didn't want.

Sometimes it gets tough working in the graveyard prediction shift as a strange request from a cloud but what more proof would you ask than this where the light is burning?

Let's swing around the sun now through the beat thrumming, drumming: there's movement but it's all so still from an afternoon nap to wake up and feel something like doomsday, like an abandoned lover, like a well-used pair of old boots, like a coffee and a smoke, like an exhausted note on a saxophone, like, it's all going away, like, it's today, like, no one calls here anymore.

So I took a boat out on the sea of it all in the moonlight and called out: "wake this moon sinking like a worm from all these holding bags of desire for the sigh is a holy sailor, sailing..."

But how do you move an earthquake?

"Ah," says the secret, "I know you now: take the number 11 bus to nowhere."

But I saw your lips move saying there's a lot of beauty around just on the tip of my tongue that's the minimum of hungry but I'm down to one thought an hour so more coffee for dropping broken lines of stray thought into cold rusty poems to find it all a pale reflection as I travelled back along the shore in the moonlight with trees casting shadows.

I went under bridges so dark and eerie and past a waterfall so noisy with the river swirling along, black and silent taking the falling leaves of this poem crashing through 3 am going strong with white hot lines driving through the dark and things flashing by and by and by from the bottom of a rusty old river that said: here's an old dog sitting in a room, waiting for a bone and there's a mile an hour of this place that has no reason because it's on fire and the lines are straight telephone wires of maybe for the fool and the pirate queen in the electrifying place that raises a roar as the revolt flares, and the ghost comes about, turning with the winds of the east to go west.

There are rumours in the air and white butterflies on the carpet and tall tales that tell of too many people living in the mountains saying there is always time for dreaming, but the daisies, the laughter and the sunshine one day at a time waiting for the feeling to come said otherwise.

And this is a river that has no end and this is a boat on the river walking a poem from a mountain in midnight walks.

Sometimes in a very special way we are connected to something more than ourselves and it is at these times that we feel holy, or in a state of grace and at other times we go chasing the moon.

A thousand very tiny men came by to say hello and brought with them a thousand healing prayers of forgiveness. The night winds were blowing with blooming messages all over the place as secret friends came and went in between of it all full of stunning desires to be.

Women called to be laid, as was their thing. I was smoking an old cigarette that couldn't get laid.

It was a night of a pantheon of a thousand failures and they were all coming at me. I wanted to go home but I could not find it. I wanted my friend but I could not find my friend.

So I slipped out in the squares of midnight where the cold rusty pavements have doors that are secret and the dreary sky has dreams to dance to break open the sky; to dance through the rain to the other side; to dance in the colour of the moon.

Oh and by the way, it has been mentioned to me that the best time to die and go to Heaven is on the 7th of March because that is when God goes on holiday and Saint Peter is not so strict and is easier to get past.

It has also been rumoured that the night watchman can be bribed and has a key for a side door, but of course you must verify these statements for yourself.

Hanging about in the graveyard won't get you very far and may even be a waste of time, and don't go writing any official letters or you could spoil it for the rest of us that want to get in the back way.

I suggest you send a few discreet whispers here and there and see what comes back at you, but don't believe all the echoes and stay away from strangers with red tails.

You know, all this started when I was a penny whisker in a farthing machine where I found myself just like anyone else stealing across the rocket of life and maybe this is the way it all goes but sawdust is the shape of this in the difference of something in my happy place where a silent noise of this page of nothing flutters out of nowhere.

"Hoot..." said the dust.

This story was as big as a thumb with holes in it and I was impressed that each kind of sadness that cast its spell and each sun that knew its own pain was a storm I had to cross to get home again where some days I died too soon and felt so apart from it all.

So I said to myself to just leave it open, for there's no time here between the dust of the moon and the time that is endless; and so this is enough of where I came from.

When you think you know how it all goes: you don't.

Every ounce of forward movement is accompanied by a huge push into the unknown.

Call me in the morning when the sun emerges to wake me from my dreams then let my fast be broken to revive me to the day.

Let not the heavy thoughts intrude too much where I would play, once more set loose in the light.

Yes, when the day comes breaking to reveal its secrets and the night's turnings have been put away, that's the time I will come to find myself, to rise and be anew.

So lend me no sighs today as oft would be the case, simply take this spirit and carry it where it would go to exchange time's dust for smiles and laughter and silences to fill me big as a cathedral in awe.

And then the rocket came to take me away.

THE DARK NIGHT OF THE SOUL

The dark night of the soul can be a wild ride full of promises of redemption and the best cure to save you where the burnt innocence of your love reaches for you on the other side of the broken bridge of dreams; and all words fall in the failure you see yourself as; and one by one all the promises turn to dust right before your eyes in the unfolding of your life as it comes to you to be burnt and to step out of the ashes anew like the phoenix rising to fly; but the weight of your darkness is a pressing need and holds you within its embrace until it has been fully consumed from within.

And then raising up you can see the first stepping stone across the river of despair; and taking it you find another and another; and it seems to any that look that you are walking on water for only you can see what is revealed to you as you step out along your way.

Your old life will call you to come back to safety and comfort, but it is not there anymore, it never really was, it was only a dream, a passing illusion you were caught in until your heart said: 'enough,' and would know the real, and breaking the bonds call out the heart-felt plea: I want to know.

Into the unknowing the answer will come, to look within, to turn from the illusion of all outward appearance and forms and find the peace you are looking for; it was always there, inside, buried under all the stuff of accumulating.

But it is a road of courage where all comes to you at the right time; and looking ahead see only the impossible and give up and take tranquillizing drugs or some other numbing substance and so fall beside the road and are carried off to the care home for the broken and lost.

Those who go through it and come out the other side stronger with a different perspective on life live more in the now than ever before.

Feel the pain, don't fear it, and don't give up even when there seems no path is before you, the path will appear and form when you are ready to walk it.

In that dark night where the soul seeks an answer and the pain is too enormous to bear and tears roll too free and solitude is where you cry from there is only one place left to go.

Into that pit then where your heart is calling. And questing down through the layers you find even fear must be left behind with all else until you arrive where you are no more to meet what isn't there and can never be yet is everything, and the joy will be great.

Stay silent, be nothing in this place; one thought here is a command to the universe and will be instantly acted upon; better to remain silent and let the love fill you, where all pain vanishes in that light.

But if thoughts come then back you will go.

Let the mask dissolve with no fear and shine for all you are worth. All words break down in the face of this and the dance begins.

AN INDIAN NEWT FULL OF SUGAR

Cultural identity could be likened to mass hysteria. All form being illusion and not real and any identity with it is a kind of hypnosis such as the old boys school of us and them and so identifying with this is a form of slavery.

Realization of this is a step towards freedom and self independence away from all forms of control.

In that independence the muddied waters clear and a profound stillness occurs and is a self awareness of being that can bring great joy; but for most the school of thought is that a fancy face can go further than being half in or half out and then some between the sheets of a full bloom; but like the poor proton in the machine of the experiment blasting off is not all it's cracked up to be before sundown with a camera in your hand when the quarks are around; and now by the miraculous decision to expand we shall presume to be innocent unless questioned guilty; this is a hot-seat you can't win so plead the fifth amendment and say nothing.

This is where we occur, where we appear and most often where we are and we shall clap for the winners who have won for no reason at all but that we've let them for they've come from the hard place and must win at all costs, and it's all right, we don't mind at all; do we Miss Jones? And if we sleep forever don't wake us, we are sound where we have fallen, peeling onions in the graveyard-shift of open expansion...

Cupid's lips but this is all a typhoid fever of beauties me bucko that is the all of it all, but you are all too late and far too soon in this awakening that can't go on without you and the heart to do so, and no one else can realize you but you.

And now the fifth dimension comes to ruin a perfectly good plan I have to run into the story lines of what I have seen to say more; but I am full of erudite like a prized Indian newt full of sugar that stands without, wasting to go within, and wishing, and I am ready to fall like a

Newtonian apple right out of the sky into those quantum arms and disappear into them forever; but how can I fall that far from here where I am on the ground with no falling beneath me?

If you look closely enough through the walls you can see patterns of energy. These patterns have edges that speak, but so far all they've said to me is that the Russians are coming with their machines that can read minds and even make you think things.

I keep asking these patterns if they can be more precise but they won't say any more, for now it seems, so I am left here to my own devices with half of an answer to all things.

LAST WORD

On another tack where the winds blow fair there is great understanding to be had that everything's going to plan, so they say, but the see through lies they tell that they say they believe in are unpalatable and this is part of the reason the whole world is rising up against them and though this uprising is commendable it is in itself not going to overthrow the corruption enough to end it.

Because we are all a part of each other in some way this corruption is a part of us all and has to be ousted from our deepest core before it will finally dissipate.

There are enough of us now to do this, inside and out and it is plain to see they are running scared of our rising in the face of so much doom.

This is our time to find the core of our being to join together in our humanity and finally make that stand for what is right.

In the power of so much light no darkness can stand against it and must surely wither way and be gone forever from the face of our beautiful Earth.

The heart-store for beauty clothed that way for mercy to take our breath away and give it back again new.

In this our dreams are pure to be where that wind blows them; a thousand lifetimes made anew in every moment of that waking are shed for our wings to grow.

And rising we find our love and know it as not separate from the whole where in great kindness we are welcomed home again.

www.ingramcontent.com/pod-product-compliance
Lightning Source LLC
Chambersburg PA
CBHW062342280526
45787CB00012B/552